D1736484

LAW ENFORCEMENT—
THE MAKING OF A PROFESSION

LAW ENFORCEMENT–
THE MAKING OF A PROFESSION

*A Comprehensive Guide for the Police
to Achieve and Sustain Professionalism*

By

NEAL E. TRAUTMAN, M.S.

*Formerly, Training Supervisor
Winter Park Police Department
Winter Park, Florida
Founder and Past President
Florida Police Training Officers' Association*

CHARLES C THOMAS • PUBLISHER
Springfield • Illinois • U.S.A.

Published and Distributed Throughout the World by
CHARLES C THOMAS • PUBLISHER
2600 South First Street
Springfield, Illinois 62794-9265

© *1988 by* CHARLES C THOMAS • PUBLISHER
ISBN 0-398-05459-2
Library of Congress Catalog Card Number: 88-476

With THOMAS BOOKS *careful attention is given to all details of manufacturing
and design. It is the Publisher's desire to present books that are satisfactory as to their
physical qualities and artistic possibilities and appropriate for their particular use.*
THOMAS BOOKS *will be true to those laws of quality that assure a good name
and good will.*

Printed in the United States of America
Q-R-3

Library of Congress Cataloging in Publication Data
Trautman, Neal E.
    Law enforcement — the making of a profession: a
comprehensive guide for the police to achieve and
sustain professionalism/by Neal E. Trautman.
        p.   cm.
    Bibliography: p.
    Includes index.
    ISBN 0-398-05459-2
    1. Police administration — United States. 2. Po-
lice professionalization — United States. 3. Law enforcement — United States. I. Title.
HV8141.T7 1988
363.2′0973 — dc19   88-476
                                                        CIP

Dedicated to
every police officer in America
who wears a badge because
he wants to make a difference

PREFACE

THE EVOLUTION OF American law enforcement has been filled with turmoil, controversy and triumph. Those having chosen to become police officers are truly special. Their lives are engulfed with daily doses of misery, frustration and tragedy. Though usually dealing with society's lowest forms of humanity, when they are with good people, it is usually during their worst moments. At the same time, the experiences of an officer also include memories of caring, helping and gratitude.

As much as the author would like it to be, law enforcement does not currently deserve to be recognized as a profession. It has yet to pay the price. *Law Enforcement — The Making of a Profession* provides the road map upon which police administrators may travel to professionalism. The reader should have no misconceptions. The journey will not be easy. It is one of sacrifice and seemingly endless hard work.

The objective, then, is to furnish the knowledge and direction most useful to achieving police professionalism. The importance of a unified, cohesive effort by sheriffs and police chiefs is stressed.

Candid and realistic guidance regarding issues of most concern is provided. These issues must be confronted and resolved. The initial chapter clarifies what the terms profession and professionalism actually mean. Such an understanding can generate the solidarity of purpose the police need.

The second chapter concerns the history of law enforcement. One of the finest ways to shape the destiny of our future is to look at where the past has taken us. By investing the time to inspect the history of the police, we are better prepared to direct our future efforts. Learn from the past mistakes of others, for their failures can be the building blocks needed to build a better tomorrow.

The remaining chapters, and primary focus of the book, is the identification and application of the world's corporate expertise and collective knowledge to contemporary and future law enforcement. The policies of America's "best run" companies and Japan's cultural wisdom are revealed. Examples of how the police apply the principles of highly acclaimed texts, such as *In Search of Excellence* by Thomas J. Peters and Robert H. Waterman, Jr., are provided. The key ingredients to achieving and sustaining professional recognition are furnished.

The following issues are addressed in a straightforward manner.

- professional attitude and conduct
- standards of employment
- education and training
- the code of ethics
- management style
- human resource development
- career development
- lateral entry
- labor unions
- civic service
- community relations
- manpower utilization
- consolidation
- state and national standardization
- accreditation
- the role of the police
- technological innovation
- planning and research
- professional associations

The author wishes to acknowledge
his sincere gratitude to Laurie Trautman,
his wife, for her untiring effort and
endless inspiration during the writing
of this book.

He also conveys appreciation and
acknowledgement to Patty Durfee,
Ross Jordan and Jeff Templeton
for their technical assistance.

CONTENTS

xi

LAW ENFORCEMENT—
THE MAKING OF A PROFESSION

Chapter 1

PROFESSION—PUTTING THE TERM INTO PERSPECTIVE

FOR ONE TO truly understand the significance of achieving professional status, a thorough examination and understanding of the term, "profession," must first take place. This chapter will focus on the meaningful and practical benefits derived from a clear perspective of the terms, profession and professionalism. Special emphasis will also be placed upon the necessary characteristics of a profession, along with the internal, public and political influences which affect it.

Misunderstandings, disagreements, arguments and a wide array of opinions often ensue during discussions regarding professionalism. Although identified as being used as early as 1541 to mean "learned vocation," by 1600 the term profession was generally used to indicate an occupation by which a person earns a living.[1]

Several centuries later, relatively little change in definition has occurred. A contemporary collegiate dictionary defines profession as "(1) An occupation or vocation requiring training in the liberal arts or sciences in advanced study in a specialized field. (2) The body of qualified persons of one specific occupation or field."[2]

Such observations are at best, superficial. One needs only to reflect upon his own definition to appreciate a more complex view of the term. Accountants, physicians, engineers, attorneys and police officers are all concerned with striving for various stages of professionalism. Virtually all those who work within the aforementioned occupations prefer to look upon themselves as professionals. From a realistic perspective, the term profession has a variety of common meanings. In addition to those previously noted, the term can simply mean that one is now paid for an act he or she renders, such as a professional athlete. Perhaps the clearest ex-

3

ample of misuse occurs during the definition of prostitution as the world's oldest profession.

Setting such observations aside, the importance of the term lies in what a profession is perceived to be. Those within law enforcement understand the significance of being professional and the sense of pride the term professionalism conveys.[3]

DEFINITIONAL DIFFICULTY

Clearly, the more contemplation is given to the concept of the term, the more inadequate many definitions appear. Attempts to define the profession concept has resulted in numerous authors concluding that a precise definition is not possible. While there is even controversy over this statement, virtually all agree that considerable problems exist in formulating an acceptable definition.

Placing such emphasis on issues of controversy and disagreement does not preclude points which most agree upon. First, no single characteristic or aspect appears to adequately define the term profession. Second, a profession cannot merely be any occupation or employment. Lastly, it is important to understand that the nature of the term invites controversy because it requires a judgement of value when using it. Such terms are referred to as dilectical. Dilectical terms convey concepts and reflect the user's judgement of value.[4]

As previously eluded to, how the general public perceives the issue of professionalism and whether a particular occupation fits their perception is a realistic consideration. Furthermore, generally accepted conclusions by the public have negative and positive influences upon the endeavors of the occupation. The public's appraisal of the degree of attained professionalism adds more complexity to the definition issue.

Though public opinions generally reflect the perceptions of society toward a particular profession, such superficial views must be challenged. Whether law enforcement ever becomes a profession will remain debatable in the view of the public.

Perhaps it is merely human nature for many citizens to view work in terms of salary alone. The amount of money a person makes tends to be synonymous with "pay" and "worth." Those in society who are paid the highest salaries are often thought of to be greater individuals than those receiving less pay. Those who receive an extremely low salary may be considered somewhat worthless. These views tend to originate from historical events and traditions concerned with noble and menial tasks. If not for such views, sanitation workers might have been considered highly respectable individuals due to their contribution to the health and welfare to society. Certainly it is unfair to conclude someone is worth ten times more than another simply because his salary is ten times greater. Such statements will remain idealistic because similar subconscious evaluations are made daily.[5]

As we come closer to deriving a multidimensional definition of profession it becomes clearer that the term is highly associated with social status. For law enforcement to achieve professional status, we must first understand the characteristics of a profession.

CHARACTERISTICS OF A PROFESSION

To fully appreciate the nature of a profession, we must examine the characteristics which comprise it. The following should be viewed by the reader as a set of minimum characteristics. The reader should not conclude that additional desirable traits do not exist. A total composite of characteristics are seemingly endless.

Any one characteristic is seldom unique to law enforcement. The so called "learned professions" such as law, medicine and theology are often used as models for standards for others to follow. These professions are considered the first "true" professions and have been widely recognized as such. They have continued to be thought of as professions over an extended period of time due to their highly identifiable and accepted characteristics. Though the road will be long and difficult to follow, the only obstacle preventing law enforcement from achieving status as a profession is the lack of tenacity and hard work. Adhering to the following set of characteristics will ensure law enforcement is a respected profession.[6]

Formal and Informal Community Sanction. A profession requires formal and informal community sanctions of its powers and privileges. Sanctions may be thought of as the manner in which society provides a profession with the power to determine appropriate curriculum, and the character of training and/or certification process. Minimum law enforcement state certification procedures and the national accreditation process are examples of such sanctions. While state certification and minimum standards have become somewhat routine, the national accreditation process remains in its infancy. Considerable resistance to the accreditation has been given by those steadfast in continuing with an insecure and unproductive manner of thinking. Those administrators who refuse to propel their agencies toward highly standardized and proficient operations are obstacles to the making of a profession.

While future reference will be made to the fact that state certification standards must be substantially raised, an appropriate perspective may be achieved by comparing law enforcement certification standards to those of other occupations and professions. Established professionals such as physicians and attorneys require a substantially higher education and/or training standard than does law enforcement. Other careers such as that of a beautician or barber may not be considered a profession though they often receive a higher degree of training and certification than law enforcement officers. There is certainly nothing wrong with being a barber. However, I question the logic of officers who feel law enforcement shouldn't increase its training and education standards when barbers must undergo two or three times that of the average officer.

Progressive Nature. A second professional characteristic is possession of a progressive nature. A profession must be perpetually innovative and progressive. Without this initiative it is destined to become stagnant and isolated within itself. A progressive nature is derived only when those within a profession display a professional tone and attitude. The desire for self-analysis and constructive criticism will yield high returns in quality.

High Ethical Conduct. What can be more devastating to the professional status of law enforcement than for the citizens of a particular community to pick up the daily newspaper and see headlines of police corruption or abuse? All professions have a high code of standards which is strictly adhered to. The failure to do so will wittle away creditability and respect until it is nothing more than a meager way to get a paycheck.

The first step in developing a highly respected ethical standard is to implement a code of ethics. The following code of ethics has been formally adopted and agreed upon by American Law Enforcement.

LAW ENFORCEMENT CODE OF ETHICS

As a Law Enforcement Officer, my fundamental duty is to serve mankind: to safeguard lives and property; to protect the innocent against deception, the weak against oppression or intimidation, and the peaceful against violence or disorder; and to respect the Constitutional rights of all men to liberty, equality and justice.

I will keep my private life unsullied as an example to all; maintain courageous calm in the face of danger, scorn, or ridicule; develop self-restraint; and be constantly mindful of the welfare of others.

Honest in thought and deed in both my personal and official life, I will be exemplary in obeying the laws of the land and the regulations of my department.

Whatever I see or hear of a confidential nature or that which is confided to me in my official capacity will be kept ever secret unless revelation is necessary in the performance of my duty.

I will never act officiously or permit personal feelings, prejudices, animosities or friendships to influence my decisions. With no compromise for crime and with relentless prosecution of criminals, I will enforce the law courteously and appropriately without fear or favor, malice or ill will, never employing unnecessary force or violence and never accepting gratuities.

I recognize the badge of my office as a symbol of public faith, and I accept it as a public trust, to be held so long as I am true to the ethics of the police service. I will constantly strive to achieve these objectives and ideals, dedicating myself before God to my chosen profession...law enforcement.[7]

Simply establishing a code of ethics does not ensure it is adhered to. A major fallacy exists in contemporary supervision and in-service training because the principles and ideals upon which the adopted code of ethics were structured are not continually reinforced. Thus, if the moral fiber upon which a profession loses its meaning, the structure of the profession is weakened. The percentage of officers who could repeat the majority of the law enforcement code of ethics that they are sworn to abide by is probably very small.

Another crucial component is the dismissal of those who abuse and misuse law enforcement power. An agency administrator will sometimes terminate an officer by forcing him to resign in lieu of being fired. When the officer resigns, the concerned administrator has done an injustice to his fellow agencies. The concerned officer leaves the agency without a blemish on his record and is then hired by another agency. He then frequently commits the same type of misconduct. Administrators have a responsibility to carry out terminations in a manner so that other agencies will be alerted to previous conduct.

Some states have taken great strides in developing procedures which revoke or decertify the state-wide law enforcement certification authority provided to officers. Florida is recognized as a leader in the area of certification/revocation procedures. The Florida Police Standards and Training Commission convenes regular revocation hearings where the concerned officer may present evidence refuting any claims which may or may not justify revoking his basic certification to be a police officer in

Florida. At the conclusion of the several month process, the revocation board decides whether to revoke certification.

Unfortunately, refined revocation or decertification procedures are not common across the nation. No profession can afford to allow dishonest, abusive or corrupt members to continue employment. Simply terminating such officers so that they can be unknowingly hired by another agency can not continue. Until effective procedures are adopted throughout America, headlines of police abuse and corruption will not decline.[8]

Education and Training. As previously eluded to, contemporary law enforcement does not have standards of education and training even close to other vocations which society generally considers professions. For decades, highly respected nation-wide commissions and organizations have been recommending that law enforcement agencies establish minimum college level education requirements for entry level police officers. Very few agencies have done so.

The most common justification for not establishing a two year or four year college degree employment standard is that agencies would be unable to hire many good individuals simply because they have not attended college. This viewpoint ignores the fact that those same individuals would most likely have been prompted to obtain a college degree if that was the accepted educational standard. In addition, the benefits of employing more educated officers are frequently underestimated. Possessing a college degree does not necessarily mean that someone will be a good police officer. It does indicate that an individual has a relatively high degree of perseverance and tenacity. It also ensures he has been subjected to a wide array of views, attitudes, opinions and facts about the society he will be sworn to serve and protect. Lastly, one of the most troublesome weaknesses in most departments, the ability of officers to effectively write, would be vastly improved.

In-service and advanced training must also be held to a high standard. States are now adopting mandatory in-service training requirements. This is certainly a step in the right direction. A decade ago in-service training for many departments was basically non-existent. Today, most agencies have some degree of regular in-service training. Contemporary in-service training issues now concern the quality of training.

Like many seemingly adverse circumstances, the current litigation climate is having a positive side effect. It's now forcing law enforcement agencies to evaluate and improve their supervision and training programs. Agencies are being forced to examine problems such as negative employment, retention, failure to supervise and lack of or improper training. Both internally and among neighboring communities, law enforcement is exchanging ideas and techniques of improvement.

Service to Society. A profession's primary purpose should be to serve a given societal need. The goals and objectives of the agency must respond directly to community needs. All true professions serve society beyond their own interests. Professions are more than occupations or vocations, partially because they do not reduce themselves to merely personal ambition or self-interest. Those within a profession pursue goals and objectives based upon the highest ideals and commitments within their reach.[9]

A profession must possess leadership which lifts it above the mundane and provides an aspect of notability. Without this leadership, a profession tends to "undo" itself. There must be a never-ending process which includes the cultivation of personal and organizational qualities and the preservation of the ideals of honor and respect. The importance of being committed to the service of one's community must be ingrown within every member of an organization.[10]

While increased professionalism will provide law enforcement officers with improved financial livelihood, our most valuable asset is the trust society has vested in us. As professionals, our highest responsibility is to discharge that trust honorably. It is a commitment no officer can ever forget.

Formal Society or Association. A widespread belief exists that an essential characteristic of a profession is the existence of formal associations and societies. A natural sense of unity always occurs when individuals share common goals, interests, educational backgrounds, problems and missions. The sense of need for a unified and cohesive group is often initiated by thoughts of establishing ethical standards, providing continuing education programs and publishing newsletters for the profession's members. Professional societies and associations assist to further the goals of betterment to society. This type of association has a purpose quite different than that of a union. A union's direct responsibility is to benefit individual members, not the community or society. It's simply the nature of a profession for its members to have a more extensive adult socialization process than members of an occupation.[11]

Unique Culture. Every profession develops a culture unique within itself. Law enforcement does not have to strive to develop this type of characteristic, a culture has developed naturally. A sense of alienation, particular terminology, internal role models and a high level of involvement has fertilized law enforcement's culture growth. It appears as though the more a profession's culture is developed, the greater the social distance between the profession and society. A professional culture results in a direct alienation between the professionals and the rest of the public, since only the professionals are knowledgeable of the internal culture.

Public Recognition. Being recognized as a profession by society is truly an essential ingredient for the making of a profession. The public generally believes that law enforcement is capable, dedicated and efficient. Whenever an agency fails in its responsibilities and can no longer maintain a set standard, public support will soon lessen. Without public support, any agency will become vulnerable to unethical conduct and inept performance.[12]

Society entrusts a bond of faith in the police to maintain law and order. Tremendous responsibility and authority rests in the hands of law enforcement. The enforcement of society's laws is the instrument of justice and framework of our democratic society. Though the problems of social discipline will only increase as America reaches higher levels of affluence, preserving and maintaining realistic principles of conduct are necessary. Just as maintaining principles of conduct are necessary in society, they remain essential to the professional growth of law enforcement.

How the public perceives a profession or occupation, striving for professionalism, is essential to both achieving and sustaining professional status. No matter what degree of professional criteria, standards or internal certification procedures are established, there would certainly be an emptiness, knowing that those outside your profession do not consider you as a professional. Whether one acknowledges it or not, the public's role in determining a profession is substantial. Certainly some of the world's finest artists have remained virtually unknown. Unsung heroes are a daily occurrence. Many of the greatest books in history have never made a best seller list.

How the public develops its perceptions as to whether or not groups are professionals is based primarily on superficial images. Television, movie productions and the manner in which a traffic ticket is issued are typical components of their opinion. The exact extent to which public recognition determines or affects a professional status remains debatable. Additional research would be helpful in resolving this question.[13]

POLITICAL INFLUENCE

The development of American law enforcement was anything but smooth and uneventful. The 1800's was a time of reform throughout most of the United States. For the police, however, only when citizenry became outraged over shocking crime waves did reform movements appear. The election of police chiefs often met with an undesirable influence of politics that spread throughout the entire agency. With the adoption of civil service in 1903, a tool was forged to take police appointments and employment out of the reach of politics. Police promotions began to be appointed through a civil service system of merit and open examinations.

As a branch of government, contemporary law enforcement is and will always be affected by politics. Federal, State and local agencies are directly and indirectly influenced on a daily basis by political occurrences. Failing to believe that politics has a dramatic influence on virtually any profession is simply naive. Understanding the nature and method through which political influence operates assists in guiding professional growth.

For the sake of discussion, the definition of political influence will include more than the activities of organizations within public office. The realities of power at any level suggests that tremendous influence is held by individuals not in public office. Within any given organization, intricate and complex politics occur daily. How chief administrators choose to allow both internal and external political influence to affect their agencies will directly influence the agencies' productiveness. The best approach is to control its influence in every manner possible.

This is not to infer that politics is always bad. It is merely a reality of life. Certain occupations and professions are affected more than others due to the nature of their endeavor. Though failing to acknowledge political influence is naive, it is not naive to always strive for the highest ideals and ethics obtainable. Police officers can never lose sight of this. Chief administrators have a responsibility to promote a professional philosophy and have a moral obligation to adhere to it themselves. How law enforcement allows itself to be affected by politics will directly influence its achievement.

PROFESSIONAL ATTITUDE

Perhaps mediocrity is, in general terms, the opposite of professionalism. Officers who settle for a mediocre police department, or convince themselves they are professional when they are not should rise above any self-serving thoughts and reassess their view of professionalism.

Professionalism is easy to recognize but extremely hard to define. One of the reasons for this is that a professional possesses a particular personality trait. No one can truly be a professional without a professional attitude. Such an attitude is a unique way of perceiving and accomplishing his or her responsibilities. It is an uncomprising pursuit of excellence.

If you have ever watched a true professional, no matter what his endeavor you've noticed a certain uniqueness in his attitude. He takes excessive pride in the quality of his work. His standards of excellence are exceedingly high, even when no one is observing or evaluating his work. A professional is the type of individual who will work to his fullest capabilities, no matter what adverse conditions are present or how he may be feeling.[14]

Having this type of attitude has absolutely nothing to do with a particular occupation or endeavor. A professional attitude cannot be awarded, adjudicated or bestowed. Many people within various occupations and endeavors are demanding to be referred to as professionals. Often, these same individuals are too busy climbing personal ladders of success to be sincere in their efforts to improve their organization. Apathy and a general insincerity toward work just are not compatible with being professional.

A professional's most important attribute is his attitude. He's the person who, when all those around him are giving up, will display uncommon tenacity. His positive view and untiring devotion will pull him through when facing extreme adversity. No matter what the endeavor, the greatest individuals in America have always had this type of attitude. Such a personal quality can not be taught. How someone feels about himself and the world in which he lives can often make the difference between success and failure, no matter what obstacles lay ahead. If someone acts like a professional, thinks like a professional and works like a professional, then he must truly be a professional.

REFERENCES

1. Morris L. Cogan, "Toward a Definition of Profession", *Harvard Educational Review,* Vol. XXIII, No. 1, (Winter, 1953), pg. 34.
2. Second College Edition, *The American Heritage Dictionary,* Houghton Mifflin, Boston, Massachusetts, 1985, pg. 989.
3. Morris L. Cogan, "The Problem of Defining a Profession," *The Annals of The American Academy of Political and Social Science,* January 1955, pg. 105.
4. Ronald C. Horn, *On Professions, Professionals and Professional Ethics,* American Institute for Property and Liability Underwriters, Malvern, Pennsylvania, 1978, pg. 4.
5. W.E. Upjohn Institute for Employment Research, Work In America: *Report of a Special Task Force to the Secretary of Health, Education and Welfare,* M.I.T. Press, Cambridge, Massachusetts, 1973.
6. Ronald C. Horn, *On Professions, Professionals and Professional Ethics,* American Institute for Property and Liability Underwriters, Malvern, Pennsylvania, 1978, pg. 8-9.
7. International Association of Chiefs of Police, *The Patrol Operation,* International Association of Chiefs of Police, Washington, D.C., 1970, pg. 2.
8. The President's Commission on Law Enforcement and The Administration of Justice, *The Challenge of Crime in a Free Society,* U.S. Government Printing Office, Washington, D.C., 1967, pg. 109-110.
9. Rosabeth Moss Kanter, *The Change Masters,* Simon and Schuster, New York, New York, 1983, pg. 53.
10. James L. Laney, "Moralizing the Professions," a speech delivered to The Atlanta Lawyers Club, Atlanta, Georgia, January 15, 1985.
11. Ronald C. Horn, *On Professions, Professionals and Professional Ethics,* American Institute for Property and Liability Underwriters, Malvern, Pennsylvania, 1978, pg. 22-23.
12. John L. Sullivan, *Introduction to Police Science,* McGraw-Hill, New York, New York, 1977, pg. 294-296.
13. Ronald C. Horn, *On Profession, Professionals and Professional Ethics,* American Institute for Property and Liability Underwriters, Malvern, Pennsylvania, New York, New York, 1977, pg. 35-39.
14. J.A. Jack, *The Boston Broadside,* The Society for Technical Communications, Boston, Massachusetts, September/October.

Chapter 2

AN HISTORICAL VIEW OF LAW ENFORCEMENT

T HE CONTEMPORARY American law enforcement administrator is faced with frequent criticism of his agency. Citizen complaints, misleading newspaper articles and insensitive elected officials are quick to pinpoint any departmental weaknesses.

The fallacy of many such accusations is that they ignore the social and political influences which often create the same problems law enforcement is criticized for not correcting. Thus, being knowledgeable of police history will allow a chief administrator to refute many criticisms by placing responsibility on the true guilty party — society.[1]

Truly, one of the finest ways to shape the destiny of our future is to contemplate where the past has taken us. By taking the time to examine our history, we are better equipped to direct future efforts in the most effective and productive manner. Learn from the past mistakes of others, for their failures can be the building blocks for law enforcement of the future to build upon.

THE DEVELOPMENT OF AMERICAN LAW ENFORCEMENT

Prior to 1800, the vast majority of America's population was from England. Because America was rural for the most part, the development of law enforcement took a great deal of time. The only law enforcement in large cities prior to 1800 was of watchmen who tended to be very lazy. There were often instances of watchmen being asleep or absent from duty.

The mid 1800's found some larger cities passing ordinances which provided for daytime police officers to replace night watchmen. As

15

agencies began to experiment with this and other basic improvements, inefficiency was prevalent.[2] Usually, a single constable kept the peace during the day. As the population of cities increased, so did the problems for police.

These were difficult times for our nation's law enforcement. The badge was looked upon in a degrading manner. Corruption and graft became widespread as political interference and manipulation grew. There were no employment standards except of size and strength. Police chiefs did not have the authority to appoint, assign or terminate officers. Discipline could not be enforced because of the political protection. Extortion of citizens, drunkeness on duty and assaulting superior officers were not uncommon. The lack of employment requirements other than political friendship also resulted in a relatively low salary. Officers wore no uniforms. The numbers on their copper badges were the only means of identification. The term "cop" originally referred to constable on patrol. An officer's 33 inch nightstick was the only weapon of defense. Political favoritism continued to flourish.[3]

State and federal levels were also growing during this time period. In 1835 the Texas Rangers organized to fight Indians, outlaws and Mexicans. The International Association of Chiefs of Police was founded in 1893 to advance the police service. The mid to late 1800's found the establishment of the United State Secret Service and the Internal Revenue Agent. The United States Department of Justice was created in 1870. The Pennsylvania State Police became a reality during the early 1900's.

Even during these relatively uncomplicated days, a few farsighted individuals realized it was unlikely for officers to become proficient unless they received special training. August Vollmer, Town Marshall and later the Chief of Police of Berkeley, California, knew a patrolman must recognize a criminal act and know which elements must be proven to convict the criminal. He believed officers must understand how and when to use force. He realized the significance of knowing how to handle people and be skilled in the art of self-defense. He understood the grave responsibilities placed upon law enforcement and appreciated the importance of training.

The early 1900's was also a time when many officers were voicing their dissatisfaction with work conditions. The famous Boston Police Strike of September 9, 1919 originated from union sentiment.

Local police unionization had begun by the turn of the century. The Boston union had requested permission to affiliate with the Americana Federation of Labor. The police commissioner refused and suspended several officers for their union activities. The union reacted by voting to strike. Thousands of officers walked off their assignments, sending Boston residents into panic.

After eight deaths, nearly a hundred injuries and in excess of a million dollars in property damage, President Wilson expressed the nation's sentiment. He stated, "A strike of policemen of a great city, leaving that city at the mercy of an army of thugs, is a crime against civilization. In my judgement the obligation of a policeman is as sacred and direct as the obligation of a soldier. He is a public servant, not a private employee, and the whole honor of the community is in his hands. He has no right to prefer any private advantage to public safety." [4]

The turn of the century was also a period of change and advancement in law enforcement technology. The bertillon measurement method of identification had been used to identify criminals since 1870. The method was considered reliable until 1903 when an individual named Will West was sentenced to Leavenworth Penitentiary. Upon arrival, an admission clerk discovered another inmate named Will West was already serving a life sentence there. To the clerk's amazement both men were virtually identical in appearance. This incident destroyed the credibility of the bertillon method and shifted tremendous significance toward fingerprint identification.

August Vollmer continued to be a domineering force toward professional advancement as he established a law enforcement training school, using the facilities of the University of California at Berkeley. In 1916, college credit courses in criminology and police related subjects were offered at the University. In 1932, courses such as first aid, police photography, basic criminal law, and police procedures were offered as a regular part of the college curriculum.

While police professionalism was struggling during the 1920's thru the 1930's, social unrest was placing great demands on law enforcement. In addition to the new Eighteenth Amendment, which prohibited the manufacture, sale, and import and export of liquor, the Volstead Act of 1919 made provisions for enforcement through the Eighteenth Amendment.

Before prohibition was repealed in 1933, it created a great deal of difficulty for the officers who were required to enforce it. When the majority of citizens ignored prohibition laws, the police became extremely unpopular. Graft, political influence and corruption substantially increased because officers were frustrated. A large percentage of the population frequently offered bribes. As the law continued its unpopularity, a general feeling of apathy toward police authority and the belief that officers could be "bought" resulted in extremely low morale and self-respect within officers' departments.

America's response to the turmoil and lawlessness of the 1920's was the creation of a presidential commission commonly referred to as the Wickersham Commission. It scrutinized virtually every aspect of the criminal judicial system. An assortment of recommendations and suggestions were developed. Many recommendations were directed toward law enforcement management and operations.

Unpopular laws such as prohibition, political influence and interference, social unrest, economic problems and an indifference to parental responsibility have always created a tremendous burden for law enforcement. Though the critics seem to ignore it, society has often been responsible for generating its own social ills. Crime is no exception. Expecting the police to control crime is ridiculous until society no longer breeds the social diseases in which it grows so quickly.[5]

In 1929 the University of Chicago offered police related courses as part of their regular undergraduate curriculum. San Jose College began to offer a two year Associate Degree in law enforcement in 1930. 1935 found Michigan State University requiring courses like chemistry and physics in their police degree program. In the same year, a safety division was created at Northwestern University by the International Association of Chiefs of Police. The division conducted research, field services and promoted traffic safety.

The rapid growing advancements in education were given an even stronger shot in the arm by the establishment of the Federal Bureau of Investigation in 1924. Organized in the Department of Justice by J. Edgar Hoover, far reaching benefits of leadership in law enforcement training and professionalism were yet to be realized. History has established that the Federal Bureau of Investigation was and will remain a leader in the law enforcement community. Director Hoover's pursuit of excellence and exceedingly high standards were tremendous examples for all to follow, during a time when American law enforcement needed a role model.

J. Edgar Hoover's untiring pursuit of professionalism was demonstrated in 1932 with the development of the Law Enforcement Bulletin. The Bulletin's objective was simply to further the advancement of the police service. It was written in a manner which provided substantial practical assistance and promoted police professionalism.

Obviously, most law enforcement agencies have attempted to hire only high caliber applicants. Each new recruit creates an image for that particular agency. America's law enforcement image received an unfortunate set back as a result of manpower shortages during World War II. The lack of qualified manpower resulted in unqualified and poorly qualified individuals entering the ranks. This era was difficult for police recruitment. Even today we live with some of the personnel procedures created then. Police personnel selection still lacks uniformity throughout the nation. There is a definite relationship between the quality of officers hired and the quality of performance within an agency.[6]

Many steps have been taken in the never ending struggle for police professionalism. As an example, the intent of establishing a civil service merit system was to provide an avenue to escape political sponsorship and manipulation. It also rewarded good merit and provided a way to appropriately deal with the problems of graft and corruption. Unfortunately, the future has shown that civil service frequently protects the inept and lazy. It often becomes counterproductive to professionalism by preventing the termination of those who should be terminated.

While the prohibition era was a time of generally poor attitude toward the police by the public, it was also a period when thousands of high quality men were seeking employment. Those who became police officers might have otherwise been lost to our profession. With an optimistic viewpoint and the proper initiative, we can frequently turn adversity into opportunity. Those responsible for recruitment took the initiative to enhance their agency by employing capable personnel. As any experienced police administrator realizes, when you start with a good quality resource, you'll finish with a high quality product.

This serge of "new blood" into the police ranks followed by a flood of World War II veterans, brought new enthusiasm and improved attitudes into the profession. New community contacts were made and increased public awareness began. The increased attention to recruitment brought about new interest in the training of those hired.

NEARING THE STATUS QUO

Law enforcement's past attempts to professionalize includes milestones such as the establishment of the Federal Bureau of Investigation's National Academy in 1935. The Academy has played a crucial role in upgrading the police service. It has trained thousands of administrative and supervisory officers from all levels of law enforcement.

The quality of any law enforcement agency is dependent upon the quality of its personnel. Therefore, it is imperative that all departments employ the most qualified officers and ensure their professional development. J. Edgar Hoover defined professional development in 1944 when he noted it to be the "Careful selection of personnel; high educational requirements; thorough training of personnel; rigid discipline; promotions based on merit; freedom from the chains of political interference; detailed investigation; appreciation of evidence; protection of the innocent; complete elimination of any semblance of any third degree tactics; unbiased testimony in courts of law and protection of civil liabilities."

The George-Dean Act of 1936 marked the first form of federal financial support for law enforcement. The act was intended to assist vocational education, however, section 6 of the act specifically provided for funds that could be used by police agencies. These early educational programs gradually evolved into college credit programs in California.

The 1940's and early 50's was an era of only mediocre professional advancement. The International Association of Chiefs of Police conducted a survey which indicated that officers throughout the nation were dissatisfied with their working conditions. Unsatisfactory working hours, salary, pension and other employment benefits had resulted in forty-four police unions in operation by 1956.[7] The late 50's marked a renewed interest in professionalizing law enforcement.

In 1959, California passed legislation establishing the Commission on Police Officer Standards and Training (POST). Its purpose was to provide technical resources, economic support and training, and educational standards to local law enforcement. The Commission was the first of its kind in America.

Almost all police tasks involve the control of human behavior. History has taught that one of the most effective ways of controlling behavior is to win compliance through laws and ordinances. A crucial training objective, therefore, is to ensure the understanding of human emotions, attitudes and drives. The application of techniques that promote a positive relationship between the community and its police force must follow. Unlike the 40's and 50's, the 1960's was a time when municipal police forces found themselves the recipient of a tide of criticism. Student unrest exploded in the streets as our nation's colleges protested social conditions and the war in Vietnam. Civil rights demonstrations became ugly and violent. Riots were almost common in some major cities. The crime rate skyrocketed. Drug addiction climbed to unprecedented heights.

Law enforcement across the country was caught ill-equipped, unprepared, and untrained during the 60's. The front line of defense against a population which increased approximately 13 percent and reported crimes that rose 148 percent was struggling to keep its head above water. Serious crime increased at a staggering rate; aggravated assault was up 102 percent, robbery rose 177 percent, forceable rape climbed 116 percent during the decade.[8]

The mid 60's crime surge resulted in a staggering amount of research. Released in 1967, the President's Commission on Law Enforcement was a two year study by more than 250 advisors, consultants and staff members. An incredibly extensive collection of surveys, reports and statistical information resulted and is used as a resource even today. While some police departments now provide police service consistent with the recommendations of the Presidential Commission, not until agencies comply with substantially increased standards of service and performance will the police become professionals. Until that time comes, the struggle for professionalism will continue.

An indication of how badly police training was needed during the 60's is acknowledged in the International City Management Association's municipal yearbook for 1968. The yearbook reported police recruits received no training in 7 percent of all central city agencies, no training in 11 percent of suburban agencies and no training in 32 percent of independent city departments. These statistics were for municipalities of 10,000 persons or more. In smaller cities less than 50 percent of new recruits received any police basic training.[9]

Until 1959, no state required basic police training. Thirty-three states had passed some form of basic training standards by 1970, but only one state specified the minimum of 400 hours recommended by the President's Commission on Law Enforcement Administration of Justice report on police. By contrast, in Germany, a two year period of training is required before an officer can be assigned to field duty.[10]

Higher education in law enforcement during the early 60's was sporatic at best. Estimates suggest that only fifteen to twenty-five colleges and universities were offering any type of full-time law enforcement program. J. Edgar Hoover exclaimed in 1964 that "More states should be making available essential police training. More universities and colleges should be initiating and increasing courses of study oriented toward the development of a career police profession. Law enforcement must raise its sights, broaden its outlook, and insist on a higher caliber of performance."

Police professionalism was truly struggling during this period. Many police agencies failed to ensure their officers knew basic criminal justice skills necessary to perform the most elementary duties. An even greater lack of advanced training was prevalent. Most departments were forced to place the emphasis on surviving in the street rather than an effort to professionalize.

There was no doubt then as there is none now that specialized training should be a prerequisite for management or supervisory positions. The police service had failed to develop proper promotion systems. Internal politics and too much reliance on the theory that "the cream will rise to the top" were common.

A study by the International Association of Chiefs of Police during the 1960's revealed the typical police officer had received less than 200 hours of formal training. This figure is a disgrace when compared to other careers. Barbers receive more than 4,000 hours. Embalmers receive in excess of 5,000. Teachers receive more than 7,000. Lawyers, more than 9,000 hours. Physicians receive more than 11,000 hours. If states and accreditation boards did not require professionals such as lawyers and teachers to meet standards of training, unqualified personnel and poor quality performance would be prevalent across America. Through requiring licenses and setting high training standards, states ensure that these professionals are confident and capable of providing high quality service. Fortunately, the number of police college and university programs increased dramatically during the late 60's and early 70's.

Since the Wickersham Commission in 1931, there has been a gradually increasing emphasis on formal education as a means for professionalizing law enforcement. Lyndon Johnson established the Commission on Law Enforcement and the Administration of Justice in 1965. The Commission recommended in the 1967 publication, "The Challenge of Crime in a Free Society," that police immediately require a baccalaureate degree for supervisors and work toward the same goal for patrol officers. The Law Enforcement Assistant Administration and The Omnibus Crime and Safe Streets Act were born from the Presidential Commission. America's "war on crime" was declared. Nearly eight billion dollars was directed toward the battle against crime from 1968 thru 1978.

The goals and standards set forth in "The Challenge of Crime in a Free Society" series called for monumental changes and implementation of many new programs to further professionalism. Some innovative and progressive police administrators initiated similar standards and goals at the state and local level, yet the impetus soon diminished. When fellow administrators did not join the movement, what had been accomplished soon died away.

A desire to increase law enforcement's general effectiveness and improve its professional stature influenced the growth of college education during the 60's and 70's. On the federal level, the rationale that a higher standard of education would contribute greatly to enhance crime control prevailed. The government felt that an improved working knowledge, expertise, initiative, and integrity would result throughout the nation's police officers.

The Veterans Administration followed with additional funding for law enforcement. Although no exact records were available at the time, an estimated figure for the year 1975 is between 58,000 and 70,000 individuals who received Veterans Administration funding were within the criminal justice program.[11]

Funding and financial concerns have always been of vital importance for law enforcement. One method of saving money has been the development of law enforcement services by contract. Some smaller municipalities make a contractual agreement with the county sheriff. The West Coast experienced the most widespread contractual use. The Los Angeles County Sheriff's Department, as an example, was contracting its services to thirty-two cities as long ago as 1970. The charge to a contract city for law enforcement services depends upon the amount of services the city requires.

The debate over contracting and consolidation of police services has and will continue for some time. Many police chiefs are adamantly opposed, stating the level of service would decrease. Some cities that have contracted for services eventually re-established their local police department. Still others claim it is the way of the future.[12]

The Law Enforcement Assistance Administration (LEAA), which evolved from the Federal Office of Law Enforcement Assistance (OLEA), provided America's major financial support for law enforcement. OLEA awarded a series of grants for the development of criminal justice curricula during the mid 1960's. In 1968, following the passage of the Omnibus Crime and Safe Streets Act, LEAA was merged with OLEA. The law enforcement educational program was established by LEAA to provide financial assistance for police officers to attend college. 1969 marked the first year that LEEP funds began distribution throughout the nation. The relatively small sum of 6½ million dollars was granted. By the mid 1970's this figure had risen to approximately 40 million dollars annually. LEEP funds continued through 1981.

Less than 500 higher education programs participated in LEEP programs during its initial six months of operation. The level of participation throughout the nation rose dramatically to reach a high of 1,065 during the year 1975. By the end of LEEP funding in 1981, the number of participating institutions had declined to just under nine hundred.

Most university and college students participating in the LEEP program were already employed by law enforcement agencies. During an average year, over 77,000 students were receiving a college education through LEEP funds. Grants were awarded to officers for payment of books, mandatory university fees, and college tuition. Funding was extremely attractive for all in-service law enforcement officers. In addition to the grants, those in-service personnel who were also attending universities on a fulltime basis, could receive up to $3,300 dollars in loans if they could demonstrate a relatively severe financial need. Both loans and grants were paid by the Federal Government at a rate of 25 percent per year. If a student resigned from law enforcement he would be subject to reimburse the remaining outstanding loan or grant.[13] Police took great strides in adopting technological advancements during the 1960's. Record systems and clerical functions were updated greatly. Crime scene capabilities were revamped. Forensic laboratories were equipped with relatively sophisticated equipment. Technological advancements in patrol vehicle computer based information systems and dispatching centers were taking place rapidly during this era.

1965 marked the development of the National Crime Information Center (NCIC). By 1967, NCIC was alive and running. Nationwide computerized information concerning wanted persons, stolen vehicles, stolen property, etc., was now available to the nation's officers. NCIC also spurred on the creation of similar information systems at the state and local levels.

The law enforcement Assistance Administration initiated the movement to equip patrolmen in many areas of the nation with small transceivers/receivers so officers could leave their vehicles without losing their communications ability. This, of course, was a tremendous help in "surviving the streets." Another area of advancement was the use of helicopters and airplanes for patrol and investigative work. By the end of the decade, hundreds of police aircraft owned by municipal, county and state agencies were in service.

As the 1960's came to an end, the social troubles which plagued all police agencies had prompted extensive internal improvements for the same agencies. Education and training levels for law enforcement officers advanced significantly. Technology was implemented and leadership was strengthened. Though it was one of the most difficult periods for the police, it was also one in which tremendous advancements were experienced. One area that lagged behind the tide of advancement was training. While federally funded incentives provided a great thrust for higher education, in-service training, for the most part, was merely a wish as opposed to a reality for most police officers.[14]

The National Advisory Commission on Criminal Justice Standards and Goals, in its 1973 publication, stated that 1982 should be the final deadline for adoption of an educational goal requiring all American police officers have a baccalaureate degree. Obviously, the deadline came without the goal being met. As the Commission noted, "Quality of police service will not significantly improve until higher educational requirements are established for its personnel." There is no doubt police professionalism and the quality of police service is related to the standard of education attained. A formal college education with degree recognition will bring support from many of those in society who consider formal education a major criteria for respect. The term "police professionalism" became synonymous with higher education during the 70's.

Professionalism has also been positively influenced by the insight and progressiveness of scholars. The academic community played a substantial role in a variety of extensive research and development. An intellectual foundation was established through the untiring efforts of authors such as August Vollmer, O.W. Wilson, V.A. Leonard and James Q. Wilson.

Federally funded law enforcement college programs during the 70's had dramatic, widesweeping effects on the quality of college level police education. The following chart indicates the nationwide education level in 1982.

LAW ENFORCEMENT—HIGHER EDUCATION

Education Level	Percent
Less than high school	0.7
High school	20.7
Less than Associate Degree	35.4
Associate Degree	10.9
Junior or more	8.7
Baccalaureate	13.4
Some graduate work	5.6
Masters Degree	3.8
Law degree, Doctorate, etc.	0.7[15]

While the majority of officers do not have a baccalaureate degree, most have attended at least some college. A great debate has continued since the 60's as to the value of higher education in law enforcement. The general belief that higher levels of education would lead to professionalism and increased quality within law enforcement is what initially generated the federal funding. Though the debate is likely to continue for years, most informed people conclude that no legitimate degree of professionalism will ever be reached without continued improvement in education.

The evolution of law enforcement from the status of an occupation to a profession has been the focus of considerable debate. There are those who point to the amazing accomplishments and advancements within the last few decades, yet, others alledge, police work can never be a profession due to the nature of the work itself. Tasks such as the removal of dead animals, the handling of drunks, or the relatively insignificant errands uniformed officers are required to perform are not consistent with a professional image. While such views are understandable, believing that relatively insignificant tasks will prevent law enforcement from attaining a level of professionalism, is ridiculous. All careers which society has generally accepted as professions have insignificant tasks. The practice of law provides legal secretaries and paralegals to perform relatively uncomplicated tasks. The medical profession uses orderlies and nurses to accomplish such duties. The fact that many law enforcement agencies now use community service officers to handle these tasks is an encouraging indication that we are overcoming the roadblocks to professionalism.

The future holds bright and challenging opportunities for police professionalism. There are already many law enforcement agencies that have rightfully earned the title "professional police department." Yet, most agencies have not. Those struggling for professionalism may discover fellow officers who find it fashionable to ridicule academic accomplishments, rather than take advantage of the opportunities before them. Such resistance has been gradually fading away as those with these opinions leave law enforcement.

It is true that the future holds many great opportunities for law enforcement. Whether law enforcement takes advantage of them could be a different matter. College degrees are prerequisites for many professions within society. Time honored professions demand high standards of qualification and performance. There should be no less demand on the police if police officers are to be regarded as professionals.

Police officers are required to engage in complex and difficult human behavior situations. They must be armed with more than a night stick or revolver. They must be equipped with the physical and intellectual capabilities necessary for directing, regulating and controlling a vast assortment of situations. It is utter nonsense for anyone to believe the complexity of contemporary law enforcement doesn't require more than physical power and common sense. There are those within law enforcement who still believe a high school diploma is all that is needed for an entry level education requirement.

Until higher standards of performance are established and accepted as truly beneficial, the quality of police service will not significantly improve. The first step was taken when higher education became a generally accepted part of the overall training and education process. However, an acceptance of higher education by some within our ranks, is far from having a self-imposed requirement by all within the ranks.

In 1979, The Commission On Accreditation For Law Enforcement Agencies, Incorporated, was created through the efforts of many law enforcement executives and organizations. It's goal is law enforcement professionalism through an overall improvement in the delivery of police services. Professionalism will be achieved through agencies voluntarily meeting exceedingly high standards of operation.

While there is no doubt that this relatively new surge for professionalism through a national accreditation process is a tremendously positive step toward professionalism, considerable resistance was encountered and remains. Some police administrators simply do not like the program being controlled at the national level. They propose that state control would be better. Others resent being told what to do and fear the process may soon be mandatory. These concerns are unfounded and should be overcome within the next decade.

The judicial system has placed a considerable demand upon law enforcement during the last few decades. Legal restrictions and regulations now govern the daily operations of officers throughout the nation. Though at first glance they may appear to cripple the effectiveness of law enforcement, the legal restrictions promoted professionalism through higher standards of conduct.

What the future does hold, in terms of law enforcement's efforts to become professional, can best be answered by what directions we are currently heading. While formal education received a tremendous boost during the 60's and 70's, the decline in federal funding has also brought a decline in police attendance in recent years. One factor which will make a difference is that if the police want to achieve and maintain a high level of income, they are going to be forced to achieve a professional image.

Personal, financial benefit is what spurred those who did take advantage of formal education to do so in the first place. It may be the same motivation which will spur both individual and departmental professionalism in the future.

Only when those within an agency's current administrative structure step in tune with administrators within the business world will the police function be seen as professional compared with other facets of society. Elevated educational standards alone will not make law enforcement a profession. No single factor will. The combination as described in the final chapter of this text will. Knowing the history of our past is an important prerequisite for gaining a true appreciation of the best pathway for the future. What a mistake it will be if we accept the road to mediocrity.

REFERENCES

1. George G. Killinger and Paul F. Cromwell, Jr., *Issues In Law Enforcement*, Holbrook Press, Boston, Massachusetts, 1975, pg. 41.
2. A.C. German, Frank Day, Robert Gallati, *Introduction to Law Enforcement*. Springfield, Illinois: Charles C Thomas, Publisher, 1964, pg. 57.
3. George G. Killinger and Paul F. Cromwell, Jr., *Issues In Law Enforcement*, Holbrook Press, Boston, Massachusetts, 1975, pg. 43.
4. Donald O. Schultz, *Special Problems In Law Enforcement*, Springfield, Illinois: Charles C Thomas, Publisher, 1971, pg. 43-44.
5. George G. Killinger and Paul F. Cromwell, Jr., *Issues In Law Enforcement*, Holbrook Press, Boston, Massachusetts, 1975, pg. 47-49.
6. A.C. German, Frank Day, Robert Gallati, *Introduction To Law Enforcement*, Springfield, Illinois: Charles C Thomas, Publisher, 1964, pg. 61.
7. Donald O. Schultz, *Special Problems In Law Enforcement*, Springfield, Illinois: Charles C Thomas, Publisher, 1971, pg. 45.
8. William Bopp and Donald Schultz, *Principles of American Law Enforcement and Criminal Justice*. Springfield, Illinois: Charles C Thomas, Publisher, 1972, pg. 35.
9. National Advisory Commission on Criminal Justice Standards and Goals, *Report on Police*, 1973, pg. 380.
10. National Advisory Commission on Criminal Justice Standards and Goals, *Report on Police*, 1973, pg. 380.
11. National Institute of Law Enforcement and Criminal Justice System, *Vol. 5 (Criminal Justice Education and Training)*, Washington, D.C.: U.S. Government Printing Office, 1976.
12. John L. Sullivan, *Introduction To Police Science*, McGraw-Hill, New York, New York, 1971, pg. 24-27.
13. John LeDoux, Edward Tully, J.L. Chronister and Bruce M. Gansneder, *Higher Education for Law Enforcement: Half a Century of Growth*, Police Chief, April 1984.

14. William Bopp and Donald Schultz, *Principles of American Law Enforcement and Criminal Justice,* Springfield, Illinois: Charles C Thomas, Publisher, 1972, pg. 159.

15. J.L. Chronister, B.M. Gansneder, J.L. LeDoux, and E.T. Tully, *A Study of Factors Influencing the Continuing Education of Law Enforcement Officers,* Washington, D.C.: U.S. Department of Justice, 1982.

Chapter 3

THE STATE OF THE ART

T HE RAPID pace of today's society places many demands, yet offers unlimited opportunities to any profession. Understanding law
enforcement's current "state of the art" is essential to meeting future
challenges, seizing opportunities and overcoming difficulties. Examining the manner in which other countries provide police services and how
their strategies, successes and failures compare to America will provide
us with new perspectives.

INTERNATIONAL PERSPECTIVES

Most professions have developed an internationally accepted mode of
operation and standard of conduct. While the basic nature of crime dictates that law enforcement throughout the world react similarly, many
differences also exist.

All countries have criminal activity. Just as the crime rate varies from
country to country, so does the response by police. A comparison of
statistical information is difficult due to inadequacies of reporting systems. Some countries, including the United States, are far ahead of
others in the manner and efficiency of reporting and documenting
crime. All factors considered, America has a relatively high crime rate,
while Japan has one of the lowest. Communists countries experience
considerable variance in the amount of crime, however, corruption and
fraud offenses tend to be the most prevalent.[1]

The corruption of police officers is a major concern throughout the
world. As the use of illegal drugs continues to increase within most
countries, widespread bribery and corruption associated with drugs has
grown as well. England, France and the United States have experienced

increasing police corruption. China and Japan, on the other hand, are relatively corruption free. China's independent commission against corruption has been very effective in regulating corruption and negative political influences in Hong Kong.

Police brutality is another problem most countries have in common. What may be considered a brutal tactic in one country is thought of as mild law enforcement response in another. While allegations of accessive use of force are a daily occurrence in every large American city, America's level of police brutality would be relatively insignificant in other nations. Claims of police brutality are extensive within South Africa, Hungary, Russia, Poland and other communist block countries. Brutality and corruption can often be associated with low salary levels. In a world where most countries consider themselves civilized, police brutality continues to plague many nations.[2]

Most countries have organized their police forces based upon the manner in which the country developed. Control and operational procedures of the police are often similar to the military. In the United States, as an example, police departments are a paramilitary organization.

Though the United States is frequently viewed as a world leader in supplying many services and goods, such advancements have done little for the high crime rate. Western Germany is recognized as having an extremely efficient police force. They remain superior to the United States in the application of various technology. Other countries are surprisingly advanced. As an example, the first impression of Columbia may bring to mind jungles, yet Columbia has developed one of the most advanced computerized communication systems in the world.

Just as traditional and political considerations affect the structure and operations of a police force, cultural differences may have a tremendous influence on both crime and the effectiveness of law enforcement.

One of the most dramatic examples of culture influencing crime and the administration of law enforcement is found in Japan. Japan has been long recognized as having an unusually low crime rate. Just as unusually low crime is usually considered the result of a culture which emphasizes traditional loyalty and a devotion to family values, the police subculture is based upon the formal samurai model. The samurai model stresses patriotism, loyalty and a sense of mission. These deep rooted values are embraced most closely by older police officers. Younger officers have now begun to be motivated more by salaries and are less willing to make sacrifices for the good of society or the police force. To combat this new mode of thinking, the police are now employing extensive informal/formal means of re-establishing the traditional samurai model in new recruits.

Just as the Japan police force is struggling with traditional and contemporary values, so is society. Thus, Japan's conflict exemplifies a phenomenon most countries experience; as a society's culture changes so will the operations of its police force. Contemporary Japanese youth also tend to find the samurai societal model less compelling. Some openly confront police authority and exhibit rebellion and hostility. Once again, when societies evolve, so does law enforcement, whose responsibility it is to control society.[3]

Law enforcement throughout the world reacts to crime in a variety of ways. Italian and French police organizations closely resemble the military model. Spain uses mobile squads of six officers when responding to emergencies, yet, uniform officers on foot are most often employed. Many countries use bicycles, motorcycles and vans in addition to automobiles as a mode of transportation for the police. Using visible deployment as a deterrent to crime tends to dominate law enforcement throughout the world. The concept of crime prevention is not universal, however.

The Royal Canadian Mounted Police is an example of a country choosing to combat crime through a national police force. The mounted police is responsible for a much wider range of duties than any single American law enforcement agency. As a result, American police officers would find tremendous differences in daily assignments in Canada. Some examples of Canada's larger scope of responsibility: having to be proficient in both english and french languages, reinforcement of an extremely varied assortment of laws, protection of wildlife and coastal waterway areas and an extensive air patrol division. The Royal Canadian Mounted Police handles everything from traffic to murder investigations, to protecting the Prime Minister and being the local cop in a small village. Even though they are responsible for a geographical area 6 percent larger than the fifty United States and investigate more than a half a million cases annually, their force is only the size of the New York City police department.[4]

Cooperation among law enforcement agencies in different countries has been improving. Italy's recent battle against the Mafia has been successful, yet, more than one hundred magistrates, public officials and police officers lost their lives in the struggle. Part of the success of Italy's war on organized crime can be contributed to the cooperation of federal law enforcement officials of the Americans and the Italian police.

Largely because of Italy's success, England, France and Germany have also increased their efforts against organized crime.

Another example of countries merging their abilities for the mutual benefit of all is in drug enforcement. Interpol, The International Police Organization, has recently reorganized many organizational procedures. These far reaching changes should enhance the assistance provided to agencies throughout the world. Improved intelligence analysis and dissemination are now very beneficial. As usual, a crisis brings people together. There has never been more cooperation between police agencies than has been experienced during the war against drugs.

Despite all the differences, police across the world are coming closer together in their approach to common problems. The need for cooperation has never been greater, as we live during a period when criminals travel from country to country with virtually no hindrance. As nations continue to assist each other, they will learn from each other's mistakes and implement the most successful law enforcement strategies and techniques the world has to offer.[5]

AN AMERICAN — JAPANESE COMPARISON

Making a comparison between law enforcement within the United States and Japan offers many insights and possibilities for improvement of police administration. As previously eluded to, a police department strongly reflects the society and community climate in which it exists. To a large degree, the actions of officers within a community are molded by the views of the society which they control. A thorough understanding of why a police administration operates the way it does, and officers act the way they do, is unlikely unless we thoroughly appreciate the culture of the concerned community.

Traditions have also influenced the contemporary structure of police organizations within both countries. The United States has an extremely decentralized system with considerable uncoordination and little standardization. Japan, however, has a national police system which provides both coordination and standardization of its operations. Where the national Japanese police force was created by design, state and federal law enforcement in agencies in America were developed through necessity. At the turn of the century American law enforcement was deemed to be the responsibility of the local government. State and federal agencies were established to supplement the capabilities of local communities.[5]

The Japanese National Police Agency coordinates and supervises forty-six distinct police divisions throughout Japan and Okinawa. The central government may only direct police operations when there has been a national emergency declared. The national police agency maintains an extensive network of criminal files, communications, forensic laboratories, advanced training schools and research and planning facilities.

The national police possess tremendous influence over the conduct and procedures of daily field operations, yet there are no direct supervised field operations. The agency's influence is exerted in a variety of other ways, however. First, the size of each independent police force is regulated by the agency. Second, it develops and implements virtually all training for the nation. Third, it regulates most finances and budgetary considerations. Fourth, salary levels for police officers must conform to what has been established by the national police agency.

Japan is approximately the size of California. Throughout the country are boundaries referred to as districts. Police station districts do not necessarily follow city boundaries. Larger cities may have several separate police stations. Each area governed by a police station is divided further by jurisdictions having a police box manned by several officers. Every foot of Japan lies within the direct jurisdiction of a police station. Close and frequent contact between officers and residence within the community is realized.[6]

By simply contemplating this aforementioned superficial description of the Japanese police structure, the extent of standardization is apparent. By comparison, the United States has a greater variety of operations and the quality of police services varies enormously. Most observers concur that Japan's enhanced standardization results in police operations and performance which are more efficient than that of America. While most states have some type of regulatory law governing standards of police operations, they are not based upon relatively high standards, and vary greatly from state to state.

Even though the improvements that standardization would bring to America are substantial, the Japanese police structure may not be practical for a nation the size of the United States, at least initially. It would be appropriate for individual states. However, those states which have tried to implement such standardization have met with strong local and county resistance. The resistance, unfortunately, often results from ignorance and fear of losing territorial power; not logic and wisdom.

America provides more officers per capita than does Japan. It is important to note, however, that the cost per officer is about the same in both countries. Even though there is relatively equal cost of police officers per unit of population, the Japanese are receiving far superior performance. The frequency of police corruption, police and public relations, the proportion of arrest to offenses, conviction rates and the effectiveness of internal police operations indicate the Japanese receive a much better return for their money than are Americans. Another consideration which affects performance is the fact that the Japanese spend considerably more of their wealth on the police than do Americans. If Americans spent as great a percentage of their wealth on law enforcement as the Japanese do, virtually twice the amount of funding would be available for police purposes. Such an increase in revenue would generate many additional officers. This of course, will improve both crime and arrest rates.[7] Putting future possibilities aside, the fact remains that current American law enforcement has more police officers per capita, yet, achieves lower qualitative performance.

Another revealing comparison is the manner of control exerted by the community over the police. Obviously, American law enforcement is influenced greatly by the political system. Like any governmental agency, they are accountable directly to elected political bodies and officials. This sometimes leads to irresponsibility, ineptness, apathy and the self-serving betterment of particular individuals. History has realized frequent incidences of political favoritism and corruption as a result of the political influence.

By contrast, the Japanese police force is not directly accountable to politicians and never has been. Throughout the nation, only one politician, the home minister, is associated with the police. He is far removed from direct contact with uniformed officers. Regulatory agencies called public safety commissions provide a solid buffer protection against political influence. Individual officers can remain confident and objective in their dealings with local politicians because community politicians do not affect them.

One of the fundamental principles Japanese law enforcement administrators instill within officers is that they are responsible for their own conduct. Furthermore, they do everything they can to insulate the police from community pressures, place tremendous emphasis on pride and consistantly require high standards of performance. The United States, however, prefers to control performance through a balance of police and political regulations. First line supervision is crucial to the success or failure of any police department in America. American officers do not have the self-discipline and pride instilled within them as do their Japanese counterparts. A vicious cycle ensues because the lesser degree of dedication and loyalty results in a need for increased discipline and internal affairs activities. Increased discipline then creates more alienation and hostility toward the department.

The lack of emphasis on internal pride, loyalty, self-discipline and dedication to duty continues throughout an officer's career. Contrary to the Japanese, an American academy places little importance on such training. A relatively short course instruction on ethics is almost all the training officers receive. When officers begin their career, little or no mention of these personal qualities are provided during a field training officer program. Very few law enforcement agencies offer in-service training on such subjects. This is a disgrace. The lack of foresight and a failure to thoroughly appreciate the value of these personal qualities are the only reasons for their absence.

The role which police in Japan play within society is less defined than in America. Teaching values and setting role model examples within the community is expected of the Japanese police. They also teach the virtue of laws, as opposed to merely enforcing them. By doing so, the Japanese police urge the community to do more than simply comply with the law. They compel the community to accept the principles and values upon which laws were established. This inturn, requires great character of each individual officer. The character of Japanese officers is a higher priority than merely requiring officers to perform specific police techniques and tasks.[8]

THE ROLE OF THE POLICE

While considerable differences exist between the role of American police and those in Japan, a difference of opinion also exists as to exactly what the role of American police is. James Q. Wilson gives us an insight in his definition of the police role:

"In sum, the order maintenance function of the patrolman defines his role, which is unlike that of any other occupation, and can be described as one in which sub-professionals, working alone, exercise wide discretion in matters of utmost importance (life and death, honor and dishonor) in an environment that is apprehensive and perhaps hostile."[9]

In reality, the role of contemporary police in the United States is complicated. Every officer, no matter what his rank or division, experiences both internal and external influences upon his views and decision making. Typical influences which complicate an officer's perception of his role include pressure from family and friends, strict departmental regulations, fellow officers, the local media, moral and ethical feelings and pressure from local crime victims. Pressures and influences will frequently lead to role conflicts for officers. A role conflict may occur when:

1. An officer perceives that others have different expectations of how he should act.
2. An officer is confronted with expectations which are incompatible with his own feelings and beliefs.
3. An officer has internalized a role that includes expectations which may be contradictory or incompatible to the role which has been established for him.
4. An officer believes that others have different expectations for him.[10]

Perhaps most American police officers have never had a clear understanding of the role they play in society. A great controversy and variety of opinions have existed regarding what that role is or should be. In general terms, the police role has continued to expand throughout this century. In 1967, the president's commission on law enforcement and the administration of justice, described the current role of the police in their publication *Task Force Report: The Police.*

> While each person has a somewhat different impression of the nature of the police function, based primarily upon his personal experiences and contacts with police officers, there is a wide spread popular conception of the police, supported by news and entertainment media. Through these, the police have come to be viewed as a body of men continually engaged in the exciting, dangerous, and competitive enterprise of apprehending and prosecuting criminals. Emphasis upon one aspect of police functioning has lead to a tendency on the part of both the public and the police to underestimate the range and complexity of the total police task. A police officer assigned to patrol duty in a large city is typically confronted with, at most, a few serious crimes in the course of a single tour of duty. He tends to view such involvement, particularly if there is some degree of danger, as constituting real police work. But it is apparent that he spends considerably more time keeping order, settling disputes, finding missing children, and helping drunks than he does in responding to criminal conduct which is serious enough to call for arrest, prosecution, and correction. This does not mean that serious crime is unimportant to the policeman. Quite the contrary is true. It does mean that he performs a wide range of other functions which are

of a highly complex nature which often involve difficult social, behavioral and political problems.[11]

What the president's commission on law enforcement and the administration of justice was saying in the aforementioned narrative has been confirmed time and time again by research. The truth is that most of society, including police officers themselves, perceive or prefer to believe that a police officer's fundamental role in society is that of fighting crime. The fact is, however, that fighting crime is merely one of the roles of an American police officer. His fundamental role is a blend of keeping the peace, community service and fighting crime.

Irregardless of the position an officer holds in his organization, he probably considers himself a protector of his community rather than a servant to provide community service. Virtually all imperical research indicates officers spend considerably more time providing community service than they do arresting and prosecuting criminals. This conflict of reality, versus what is perceived to be, creates a strong likelihood that the internal management of agencies may be directed to misappropriate roles. As an example, considerable training may be devoted to arrest and apprehension procedures, yet relatively little is directed toward tasks associated with community service and interpersonal relationships with citizens.

It is not difficult to understand why society demands that police officers perform a wide array of community service and peace keeping tasks, as opposed to strictly law enforcement. Requests, like assisting a citizen who has locked car keys inside his vehicle or helping an elderly lady who has fallen out of bed during the early morning hours, occur because there is no other facet of society available to help at a moments notice. A community knows that officers are always available and feel they are warranted because the community pays their salaries. This feeling has continued to grow during past decades. An officer's function and role has gradually evolved to that of a "peace officer" rather than the more traditionally concept of a cop as a "crime fighter."[12]

One may draw strong correlations between the role of an American officer and the more traditional role of the police in Japan. If we agree the role of a contemporary police department is to provide a wide range of community oriented services in addition to the traditional law enforcement role, then we must manage our organizations to fit that purpose. Misdirected internal operations will lead to a lessened degree of efficiency and effectiveness. Those who assume ultimate responsibility for developing and directing an organization are, of course, the chief administrators. A chief of police or sheriff is responsible for and sworn to take corrective actions. The failure to do so will perpetuate traditional, but less effective operations.

It would be a mistake to assume that such a redirective project is a minor undertaking. By contrast, altering long held views will meet resistance from all levels of an agency due to the popular belief that an officer's purpose is only the enforcement of laws. Those administrators who have the foresight, tenacity and courage to alter the internal structure of their organization to meet this all encompassing perspective of the police role should consider a variety of issues. An agency's research, planning, training and management components must be aligned to accept an expanded performance concept. The organization's climate must encompass an attitude of maintaining order and providing service in addition to the traditional arrests and prosecution priorities.

The current movement toward establishing community service officers to perform less complicated or demanding duties is very suitable and easily adapted to serving the majority of law enforcement's public service needs. There are those who claim law enforcement can never be a true profession because it's the nature of an officer's role in society to provide relatively menial community service oriented tasks. Tasks that a nurse's aid and orderlies perform in the medical profession. Secretaries and paralegals assume these roles in the legal profession. There is absolutely no reason why law enforcement can not strive for an expanded police role, then provide these additional services through community service officers.

Since community service officers do not respond to high risk or complicated situations, a much lesser degree of training is required. Manpower will be strengthened since regular police officers will have more time to concentrate on higher priority and more complicated occurences. Lastly, instituting a community service officer program is consistent with sound fiscal management, since community service officers' salaries are substantially lower than regular officers.

In summary, the traditional police role in America has taken a gradual and sporadic evolution through this century. The strict paramilitary structured policing system has begun to evolve into a more service oriented organization. The change has been slow and cumbersome. We remain far from where we should be. Any enlightened administrator who seeks to alter how his officers perceive their role within the community will meet resistance from his officers. This realignment of purpose cannot be implemented without a thorough awakening of attitude and role by all employees of the organization.

For the administrator with the wisdom and determination to make progressive changes, several roadblocks may lay ahead. These roadblocks can be crossed. Problems can be overcome. Any difficulties arising in the path of innovative change will only be temporary setbacks in a long line of accomplishments for such a police chief or sheriff.

THE CRIMINAL JUSTICE SYSTEM

The police, through the identification, arrest and prosecution of an offender, initiate the criminal justice process. Not only the police, but virtually every citizen in America is aware of the inefficiency, injustice and ineptness of the current criminal justice system. Frustration frequently overwhelms personnel within all aspects of the system. The police become frustrated because their efforts often appear to be in vain. Prosecutors and public defenders share the same frustration at futile attempts to deal with the system's massive volume of cases. The courts remain overworked and understaffed. Probation and parole components have similar difficulties and problems. Correctional institutions are forced to release criminals prior to anticipated release dates due to the severity of overcrowding.

There are those who claim that major changes in the criminal justice system should have occurred years, if not decades, ago. Though certainly debatable, these claims and similar allegations appear to be based upon a somewhat superficial analysis of the system. When compared to the judicial systems of other countries, America ranks high in its fairness and devotion to the preservation of determining guilt and innocence. The heart of most substantial problems of the American judicial system lies in the massive number of offenders. Our system of justice evolved from the English common law into a complicated and integrated system of procedures and regulations. The overall system is comprised of many intrasystems which are both directly and indirectly dependent upon each other. Historically, the United States constitution guarantees that certain procedures occur within the administration of the justice system. Though specific criminal cases may be handled differently in particular jurisdictions, all court decisions are guaranteed due process. Contrary to a somewhat simplified and uneducated view, the criminal justice system remains very complicated and cumbersome.

A great deal of crime is never reported to the police. When it is, the concerned police agency follows well established procedures in an attempt to apprehend the perpetrator. Very often the offender is neither identified or apprehended.

Following an arrest, a law enforcement agency must interact with various sub-systems within the judicial system. Unfortunately, most officers view their position as relatively independent from the other major components of the system. As an example, if an offender was not found guilty, officers tend to place blame with the prosecutor. When a criminal is released from prison, officers are frequently angered by the offender not having served a full sentence. Judges, penologists, social workers, prosecutors, defense attorneys and criminologists are sometimes looked upon with distain by officers who fail to understand the overall scope, purpose and mechanism of the judicial system. Local police academies and chief administrators must take it upon themselves to ensure that officers receive a more well defined and thorough understanding of how the police should interrelate and strive for improvement within the system. The problems, difficulties and restrictive hardships of other judicial sub-systems should be stressed.

An illustration of the interaction of local, state and federal governments may be made by examining employment levels of various components. As the following chart depicts, police protection is primarily a function of local government. Corrections are a basic responsibility of state government. The majority of all justice personnel in America are employed at the local level.

Percent of Criminal Justice Employment
by Level of Government

	Local	State	Federal
Police	75%	14%	11%
Judicial	66	29	5
Legal Services and Prosecution	63	27	10
Public Defense	56	41	3
Corrections	38	57	4
Other	38	45	17
Total	64%	27%	9%

Source: U.S. Department of Justice Report to the Nation on Crime and Justice, U.S. Government Printing Office, Washington, D.C., 1983, pg. 45.

Contemporary police organizations are highly decentralized both theoretically and realistically. Ultimate control over the police role is a power reserved for individual agencies and states. For the federal government to assert control over local law enforcement agencies would be unconstitutional. As eluded to previously, decentralized fragmentation of the police generates an assortment of inefficiencies. The ineffectiveness travels beyond police organizations, until the entire criminal justice system is detrimentally affected.[13]

Striving for liberty, justice and equality for all is frequently an overwhelming task. Any experienced officer knows the judicial system is riddled with problems. The police, the criminal justice system and society as a whole have been experiencing a renewed interest in making a variety of improvements in the judicial system. Some of the contemporary programs include the development of victim advocates, citizen dispute settlement programs, uniform sentencing guidelines, judicial arbitration programs, redefining rules of discovery, improved prosecutory effectiveness and increased involvement of the police within the prosecution process.

Because no other segment of the criminal justice system has as much direct contact with the public as do the police, the degree of public confidence is largely dependent upon the trust citizens have in their law enforcement officers. The contact individual officers have with the public often involves situations where officers may use discretion regarding the handling of given circumstances. Many individuals in the judicial process have the authority to use discretion. Officers must learn how to exercise their considered judgement within the guidelines set by law.

Chief administrators have a responsibility to ensure that officers under their command exercise sound, mature and thoughtful discretion. Since no one can possibly foresee all potential situations, it is crucial that a mature, professional frame of mind be instilled within the police.

Limits of the use of discretion vary from location to location throughout America. Imposing a more restrictive deadly force policy, determining sentencing guidelines and passing mandatory sentencing regulations are examples of how the criminal justice system tends to regulate the use of discretion. The following chart further defines who within the judicial system uses discretion and how they use it.

USE OF DISCRETION WITHIN THE CRIMINAL JUSTICE SYSTEM

Type of Justice Official	*When Discretion Is Used*
Police	When investigating crimes
	While searching for people
	While enforcing laws
	While detaining or arresting individuals
Prosecutors	When seeking indictments
	While filing charges
	When dropping cases
	When reducing charges
Judges	When accepting pleas
	When dismissing charges
	When determining delinquency
	When setting bail
	When imposing sentences
	When revoking probation
Correctional Officials	When assigning to a correction facility
	For disciplinary matters
	When awarding privileges
Parole Officials	When determining conditions of parole
	When determining date of parole
	When revoking parole[14]

PERSONNEL SELECTION

Undoubtedly, personnel selection is an extremely important aspect of any police organization. Those who have been responsible for the selection process deeply understand the difficulty involved in determining and selecting the best qualified available personnel. Again, the chief administrator assumes final responsibility for the consequences of personnel selection and management. In principle, his persistence to accept only the highest quality selection of personnel must be unwaivering. In reality, the contemporary chief of police or sheriff finds the assortment of personnel requirements and extenuating circumstances make the selecting of only the highest qualified personnel difficult, to say the least.

The extent to which a chief administrator has direct knowledge and control over the personnel selection of specific officers is largely dependent upon the size of the department. In smaller agencies the chief of police is able to directly oversee the selection process personally. In large departments, he rarely has direct contact with applicants due to the volume of individuals being processed.

Most municipal and county law enforcement agencies have a central personnel agency within their government. The direct control and influence these agencies have vary from jurisdiction to jurisdiction. Typically, job descriptions are regulated, minimum standards for various positions are established and entrance examinations are given and documented. Furthermore, they oversee the selection process and provide guidance to various governmental divisions regarding personnel matters.

The central personnel agency is not directly responsible for the operation of a police personnel division. For it to have such control would violate the principle that authority should not be delegated without the person or agency to which it is delegated being held responsible for its actions.[15] Frequently, a clear understanding and relationship between the central personnel agency and the personnel division of a police department does not exist. Should this arise, the administration of the police department must take quick and decisive steps to arrive at a clear understanding or serious personnel consequences may occur.

Most small or medium size law enforcement agencies assign responsibility for the employment selection process to a particular officer. It is frequently a part-time responsibility for a staff member. This is in strong contrast to a large department which has an entire personnel division to handle exactly the same matters. Whether an organization uses a staff of one or a dozen, those handling the employment process must remain confident and exhibit a strong determination to employ only the best qualified personnel.

The employment process, though crucial to the effectiveness of an organization, will continue to be a very difficult and sometimes frustrating task. Officers assigned should be provided sufficient time and manpower to execute their responsibilities. Manpower limitations often force smaller departments to assign employment processing to an officer in addition to his "primary" duty. Larger departments may have several individuals assigned to the selection process, yet be substantially understaffed. Administrators should no longer view this assignment as an area which can "get by" without sufficient manpower. Officers, who, for a variety of reasons, have been taken off the street, should not be assigned to personnel selection simply because there is no other place to assign them.

The majority of competent law enforcement agencies in America typically have the following phases within their employment selection process:

1. Recruitment
2. Application Process (including all pertinent paper work necessary for background investigation)
3. Fingerprinting process
4. Polygraph examination
5. Physical agility examination
6. Psychological examination (written and oral)
7. Thorough background investigation
8. Medical examination (to include drug screen)
9. Oral interview(s)
10. Probationary period (probationary period shall include a field training officer program)

Considerable controversy now exists concerning various aspects of the employment process. Mandatory drug screening of applicants is beginning to occur throughout the nation. Physical fitness examinations must now be job related. The validity of polygraph examinations continues to be debated. English tests are rarely given, even though they are a simple and effective manner of improving inept police report writing. The equal employment opportunity act of 1972 has induced many police departments to change their employment selection policies. Affirmative action has considerable influence over hiring minorities.

Many administrators are acutely aware of the importance of quality hiring practices. Others have chosen to ignore, or are ignorant of, its importance. An enlightened awareness of the value of quality hiring provides a sound investment in the future.

PERSONNEL MANAGEMENT

A decade ago virtually all American law enforcement agencies conducted firearms training during the day. A single stationary silhouette target was used. Firing line distances of 7 yards, 15 yards, 25 yards and 50 yards were the norm.

We now know that firearms training of the past was relatively ineffective. To become more effective and truly help officers survive, the street traditions of the past have been altered. We know that approximately two out of three police murders occur during hours of darkness. Approximately 40 percent of all police murders involve more than one armed suspect. The average distance of a slain officer from his perpetrator is 15 feet or less. Accordingly, firearms training procedures have been changed. Agencies are also increasing the frequency of nighttime firearms training. Courses which use multiple targets at distances less than 15 feet are becoming common.

An analogy may be drawn between firearms training and personnel management. In both cases, law enforcement has accepted traditional methods without question. In both instances we now understand that revising accepted procedures is crucial to safeguarding the lives of officers and to developing an efficient organization.

Revised personnel management procedures have not developed as quickly as those of firearms training. Even though most renowned management experts agree that strict authoritarian and theory x management styles do not produce the highest potential of performance from employees, few law enforcement agencies have made a true commitment to human resource management.

Until sheriffs, chiefs of police and high ranking staff members do more than simply agree that the effectiveness of their agency can never exceed the quality of its personnel, police efficiency will continue to be stifled. Without a doubt, some innovative and progressive departments have taken the lead in establishing effective human resource management programs. The majority, however, remain satisfied with outdated and stifling management techniques. Considerable knowledge can be learned by examining how the corporate world uses "state of the art" human resource management to produce peak performances from their personnel.

ASSESSMENT CENTERS

Contemporary corporate management and employment processing frequently includes the application of assessment centers in lieu of or in addition to traditional methods of selection. Just as with most employment testing procedures and promotion interviews, an assessment center attempts to predict future performance. It involves an assortment of scenarios which simulate realistic and practical performance. Multiple observers and evaluation techniques are used. Realistically developed assessment simulations produce a standardized evaluation of behavior based on multiple samples of performance.

Assessment centers are not new. The military and corporate communities have used them with great success for some time. As with the implementation of any new technique within an organization, the possibility of misunderstanding or confusion exists. Some areas having a potential for misunderstanding include:

1. *Simulations* — The simulation exercises used should realistically portray the position for which the individual is applying. They must be relevant, objective and realistic for the organizations to benefit. Typical simulations include oral presentations, inbasket exercises, common management problems, written communications, group discussions, evaluations of subordinates and simulated field exercises.

2. *Assessors* — Assessment centers should use multiple assessors. They must receive competent training prior to implementation of assessment exercises. Following the participation of an applicant an assessment evaluation meeting is held for assessors to combine their evaluation data and openly discuss an applicant's performance.

3. *Expense of Assessment* — At first glance it appears the cost of conducting an assessment center is greater than more traditional written and oral interviews. This is because multiple assessors are used and the series of simulation exercises is relatively time consuming. The cost of assessment is less than it may appear, however. The true expense of promotion decisions and entry level selection includes more than the direct cost of the manner in which the decision is made. It also involves the expense of making decisions to promote individuals to positions in which they do not perform well. The cost of making wrong promotion decisions can be staggering over an extended period of time. In summary, good police officers and supervisors make less mistakes. Money spent to make effective employment and promotion decisions will pay off in superior organization performance.[16]

CIVIL SERVICE

In an effort to reduce the effects of political manipulation and influence, the Pendelton Act of 1883 was passed by Congress. The act provided for civil service in the federal government. It made a real breakthrough for the establishment of civil service in law enforcement. For slowly, as gross political interference began to disappear, local and state governments were introduced to civil service. Today, the majority of governmental employees at all levels are civil service employees.

No one should doubt the purpose of the contemporary civil service merit system. It provides for disciplinary procedures and deals with problems of graft and corruption. It promotes ability and merit as an alternative to political influence and ensures that officers are treated fairly. It is generally considered a system that has assisted tremendously in combatting the injustice in politics.

As state and local governments continued to pass legislation establishing civil service systems, detrimental aspects and limitations were exposed. Undoubtedly, political interference is an evil which should not be tolerated. Yet, just as crippling to an organization is unjust protection of the inept. Protection of incompetent employees is a byproduct of civil service rules and regulations. As most chiefs of police can attest through personal experience, civil service all to frequently protects officers who should be demoted or terminated. The "protection" is often taken to such an extent that flexibility of administration is impossible. Common sense and logic may take a back seat to civil service regulations which were never intended to camouflage or perpetuate poor performance. What began as sincere attempts to prevent favoritism now sometimes does nothing more than hamper responsible leadership and be devastating to the overall effectiveness and morale of the organization.

The detrimental effects of civil service upon law enforcement have continued for decades. The inability to discipline or terminate officers appropriately creates numerous negative consequences. Fairness, justice and the belief that dedicated hard work will ensure the best employees of career advancement, may become a joke among officers. Successful corporations and businesses could never operate at optimum levels of performance when confidence and performance are detrimentally affected by such regulations. Though civil service still affords protection of unfair employee treatment, its negative results must not be ignored any longer.

Another major drawback of civil service is that it prohibits lateral entry throughout the nation. It is way past time for law enforcement to join the rest of society and disregard such restrictions as archaic and "out of date." Once again, we can learn from the corporate world. The business community doesn't have all the answers. Eliminating civil service, as an example, would mean eliminating a degree of job security. Yet, there are alternatives to civil service which would better serve law enforcement.

The existence of sheriffs' departments operating without civil service lends itself to the fact that law enforcement agencies no longer have the level of graft, corruption and political influence which necessitated civil service during the era of its conception. Changing from a civil service system will not be simple since legislation was required to implement it. However, those administrators who are willing to commit themselves to the struggle will find a more efficiently run organization when their efforts are concluded.

CIVIL SERVICE ALTERNATIVES

Every agency which develops a competent managerial system to replace civil service will benefit all of law enforcement, as well as themselves. From the perspective of professionalism, the undesirable effects of civil service regulations have helped to keep police officers at the nonprofessional status of an hourly employee. It's difficult to imagine physicians or attorneys being civil service employees. The police profession needs the opportunities that nationwide lateral entry can provide. It needs the ability to terminate undesirable personnel without the interference of misguided regulations. Restrictions should not prohibit a chief administrator from making personnel changes or salary adjustments as he sees fit.[17]

In summary, law enforcement needs to rid itself of the stagnation and decay which the civil service system tends to promote. Certainly it provides a guarantee of security and protection of employment. Yet, in reality some of the employees civil service protects are the inept and apathetic. In lieu of civil service, progressive law enforcement must accept only the most effective management. Efficient, strong administrators with the skills, abilities and knowledge necessary to ensure fairness, loyalty and perseverance provide the solution.

POLITICAL INFLUENCES

Politics affect virtually every aspect of daily life. With the exception of those who are naive, this is readily accepted. Every organization, from the smallest family business to the largest corporation, experiences internal politics. How an organization is affected by these influences will primarily depend on the management style within the organization.

Having even greater potential for impacting a law enforcement agency is the assortment of external political influence. Locally, the relationship of the mayor, city manager, commissioners and influential citizens frequently affect the entire organizational climate of the department. There is usually a close relationship between the community's political culture and its law enforcement agency. Irregardless of a civil service system, local politics inevitably affect the operations of any agency. Although usually assumed to be detrimental, the effect may sometimes be positive.

City or county commissioners, the city or county administrator and mayors influence the daily operations of a chief of police or sheriff just as the superior/subordinate relationship works at any level. Having the determination and courage to "stand up" for what you sincerely believe is the right decision is most difficult at the local level. The political realities of life have caused many fine administrators to suddenly discover they were unemployed. Developing a sound, professional and productive relationship with community leaders is an important, perpetual process. Those involved must never lose sight of the fact that fighting for one's convictions may have devastating career results, yet, no matter what the result, the alternative is simply unacceptable.

Even with the civil service process, the turnover rate for chiefs of police in America is very high. Most serve at the pleasure of the city manager or mayor. Those administrators with less conviction than others will yield to their perceived career danger and take action which may not be in the best interest of their department. When this happens, the fight for professionalism takes a solid blow. Any influence that stifles or stagnates fairness, professionalism and ultimately justice can not be tolerated.[18]

The implementation of a contractual agreement system may be an effective solution. Starting officer's employment through the use of a three to five year contract would be beneficial to both employee and employer. At the end of the predetermined contractual period, the contract can easily be renewed. The chief administrator can decide not to renew the contracts of unproductive officers. This policy would elleviate some of the negative aspects of the civil service system, yet provide a degree of security for competent officers. Terms of the contract would prevent termination prior to the end of the contract, unless the officer violates certain predetermined regulations.

Due to the substantial political influences at the chief of police level, ensuring that a chief's termination follows an acceptable due process procedure is critical. The termination and appointment dates of law enforcement chief administrators are sometimes synonymous with mayoral elections. The absence of tenure creates an absence of job security. An internal municipal policy providing for removal of the chief of police, only after proof of misconduct in office, should be established. A termination hearing must be based upon an investigation conducted by an

independent body. Furthermore, it must be conducted in a formal setting, and allow for an appeal process.

GOVERNMENT SPENDING

Thousands of local, state and federal governments have participated
in the Bureau of Justice statistics and Census Bureau surveys during the
last few years. The primary purpose for this data is to assist in the development and implementation of effective law enforcement and criminal
justice policies. Examining well developed data furnishes an important
insight of how we, as a society, prioritize the police and criminal justice
on the basis of financial expenditures.

In 1983, America's total spending for justice at all levels of government was less than 3 percent of the overall governmental expenditures.
Our nation spends more than three times as much for the interest payments on public debt than we do on our justice system; nearly twice as
much on the environment and housing, four times as much on education and almost six times as much on national defense.

At the local and state level in 1983, 6.2 percent of government spending was directed toward justice activities. Of this amount, 3.2 percent
was allocated for law enforcement, 1.7 percent for corrections and 1.3
percent for legal and judicial services. Financial statistics are another example of proof that criminal justice is essentially a local and state responsibility. When examining governmental expenditures from a dollar
amount, we find the nation's expenditures for criminal justice were 23.1
billion dollars at the local level. State governments spent 11.7 billion.
The federal government spent a relatively small 4.8 billion dollars.[19]

The total funding of the United States government for civil and
criminal justice at all levels was approximately 40 billion dollars during
the fiscal year of 1983. This was an increase of over 10 percent from the
fiscal year of 1982. At first glance it may be difficult to put such overwhelming expenditures into perspective. Though 40 billion dollars is an
astronomical amount of funding, it is only 2.9 percent of the total
American governmental expenditure for services.

Social Insurance Payments**	22.0%
National Defense and International Relations	16.9
Education	13.1
Interest on Debt	9.8
Public Welfare	6.2
Housing and the Environment	5.4

Hospitals and Health	4.2%
Transportation	3.4
Justice	2.9
Technology and Research	.5

Source: Bureau of Justice Statistics, Justice Expenditure and Employment, 1983, U.S. Department of Justice.

**Social Insurance payments includes unemployment compensation, employee retirement, worker's compensation, social security and "other" categories.

Though studies indicate salaries are not as important to employees as the way they are treated by management, it will always be an important personnel issue. Try telling a "street cop" with a family of five or six that it's just another personnel issue. Salary levels will rise in accordance with an increase in professionalism. Physicians and attorneys can successfully demand a high payment for service because the public perceives them as professionals. The following table notes 1986 salary levels for state police.

SALARIES NATIONWIDE

Survey of salaries for state law enforcement

	State	Minimum*	Maximum*
1	Alaska	$35,976	$50,112
2	California	27,708	33,084
3	Oregon	24,552	32,136
4	Colorado	23,784	31,860
5	Arizona	22,471	30,988
6	Delaware	22,230	29,224
7	Missouri	21,600	40,024
8	Rhode Island	21,166	29,804
9	Washington	21,264	30,720
10	Illinois	21,132	36,132
11	Ohio	21,112	27,788
12	New Hampshire	20,766	25,109
13	Oklahoma	20,400	27,336
14	Connecticut	20,301	24,492
15	Minnesota	20,254	28,856
16	Kansas	20,124	28,308
17	Texas	20,052	25,338
18	Pennsylvania	19,821	29,022
19	Nevada	19,473	26,295
20	Michigan	19,344	30,118
21	Wisconsin	18,674	28,057
22	Massachusetts	18,624	23,862
23	Iowa	18,345	25,480
24	Virginia	18,312	25,028

SALARIES NATIONWIDE *(continued)*

	State	Minimum*	Maximum*
25	Indiana	$18,174	$26,502
26	Wyoming	18,168	29,052
27	New York	18,165	29,417
28	Georgia	18,150	28,512
29	Montana	17,852	27,050
30	Maryland	17,612	23,136
31	West Virginia	17,568	21,492
32	New Mexico	17,328	23,460
33	Utah	17,163	27,914
34	Nebraska	17,148	24,577
35	North Dakota	17,040	26,040
36	Maine	16,744	21,667
37	Alabama	16,556	25,168
38	New Jersey	16,533	25,517
39	North Carolina	16,464	30,000
40	South Carolina	16,311	23,118
41	South Dakota	16,016	23,628
42	Mississippi	16,008	25,066
43	Idaho	15,766	23,296
44	Louisiana	15,684	25,572
45	Vermont	15,314	27,230
46	Kentucky	15,288	29,932
47	Arkansas	15,210	27,976
48	Florida	14,657	21,673
49	Tennessee	13,212	19,632

*Based on starting minimum salaries for 1986.
Hawaii has no state police agency.[20]

The percentage of government funding granted the judicial system is unacceptable. There has been a substantial decline of federal funding to law enforcement in recent years. Local and state governments simply don't provide enough. The immediate future does not indicate an improvement in this trend. Efforts to make the most of available resources are a logical course of action.

The influence of local politics upon federal politicians can be substantial. If local residents would demand more federal assistance in helping law enforcement curb the tide of crime, a definite potential for improved funding will exist. Local citizens, however, usually need a little encouragement from a sheriff or chief before they'll make a phone call or write a letter. A community's view of their police is much more influential than most officers think.

FISCAL MANAGEMENT

The economy has and will continue to have a significant influence on law enforcement. Personnel cutbacks, layoffs, Proposition 13, government waste and inefficiency, taxpayer revolt and a declining tax base are all phrases which strike the hearts of contemporary police managers. Chief administrators experience considerable pressure and scrutiny regarding their budgetary decisions. Although every organization has a particular uniqueness to their daily fiscal operations, certain principles may be helpful to every agency.

The 1978 passing of Proposition 13 drastically cut local property tax revenues in hundreds of California municipalities. Crisis management suddenly became a necessity. Balancing the budget with substantially less revenue and justifying the manner in which it is done is a difficult task at best.

Just as with many adversities, there have been positive side effects. Law enforcement administrators have frequently become more proficient in the daily operations of financial management. A dramatic increase in the number of professional seminars in fiscal management related areas has occured. In addition, a variety of cost effective internal programs such as improved fuel consumption driving and a reassessment of manpower allocation have been developed.

There are times, however, when even the most progressive, innovative and well researched fiscal management plans are simply not enough. As an area dependent upon the ailing auto industry, the Flint, Michigan, Police Department has suffered greatly due to economic decline. When a local economy experiences substantial financial difficulties, the livelihood of the city will inevitably suffer accordingly. As Flint police chief, Max Durbin stated in retrospect, "Before fiscal '79 was out, I had already started to cut. As early as the new year, it was obvious that the auto industry was in a pronounced recession and that we were going to have severe fiscal problems ourselves. When the ground hogs come out, can spring be far behind? We started reducing our work force in April, both through attrition and layoffs. On April 24th, I layed off thirty-three patrolmen and a number of civilians. The budget, almost 16 million, was paired to about 12.5 million."

Deputy Chief Charles Gilmore recalls Flint's efforts at making the most of its limited resources. "We did away with our community relations unit because of the fiscal problems, and we also cut back on training, but we put the officers freed by these shifts in the cruisers to answer routine calls."

Flint Police Department is not alone. Tax cuts and a poor economy will trigger a chain reaction likely to snowball into a nightmare for the local sheriff or chief of police. When a tax base shrinks, the expense of city services is likely to increase. Believing it can't happen is simply being naive. Layoffs, little or no pay increases, inoperative and outdated equipment, the lack of manpower and a demoralizing atmosphere will probably riddle an entire organization.[21]

The phenomena of local communities experiencing financial difficulties is nothing new. During the last century, thousands of local governments have defaulted on their financial commitments. Though to a large extent, the efficiency of operations within a police organization tend to shape its financial destiny, seemingly uncontrollable factors can have a tremendous influence. At the state level, there are many state mandated programs which local governments must fund. Mandated retirement benefits, disability policies, levels of training and police services must also be financed. Local city ordinances, civil service regulations, municipal charters and executive orders play significant roles in the manner of budgetary preparation and fiscal operations.[22]

Truly proficient fiscal management is a very complicated task. The degree to which chief administrators become directly involved in routine financial management often depends on the size of the organization. Irregardless of the organization's size or related considerations, all administrators should be knowledgeable and capable fiscal managers. This does not infer they should not accept other officers as capable of this complex task. The overriding single action which would most benefit a police organization is acquiring professional financial assistance.

Typically officers, having been promoted or transferred to a staff position, assume the responsibility of budgetary matters. More often than not, these officers have little or no professional credentials or financial training. This lack of expertise will naturally result in a decrease of proficiency. At no fault of their own, they just don't have the knowledge and abilities to effectively accomplish their responsibilities. When this occurs, the entire department suffers. Chief administrators can make a simple, yet, substantial, overall improvement by providing these individuals with quality training or acquiring a civilian who has the expertise necessary for the task.

ORGANIZATIONAL STRUCTURE

Law enforcement agencies are generally considered semi-military organizations. Even the youngest rookie understands the similarities between the daily activities of his department and the military. Compliance with the chain of command structure, uniforms, squads and divisions, inspections and a strict adherence to standard operating procedures and general orders are obvious military-like characteristics. In addition, a semi-military organization usually develops an attitude within officers that is not particularly conducive to developing the highest possible potential these officers have to offer.

Proponents of the semi-military organizational style note several benefits.

1. The strict adherence to policy will ensure quick and decisive response to orders in an emergency.
2. Provides for strong discipline.
3. Assists in preventing officers' personal views from influencing desicions.
4. Assists in ensuring that officers follow departmental rules and regulations.

The traditional semi-military structure adopted by the vast majority of agencies throughout America has had many detrimental effects on the performance of the police. The semi-military structure is intended to provide strong control and supervision over the actions of officers. This form of management is appropriate for a military organization because military leaders have only a single basic purpose; to lead subordinates into battle. Such a work setting calls for extreme discipline. Military personnel do not require the discretion and decision making that street officers use on a daily basis. Thus, the strict authoritarian style that's good for the military is ineffective for the police due to the need for more flexibility and freedom of decision making by subordinates.

Tradition dictates many of our accepted daily practices. Assuming a particular manner of operation is correct just because "that is the way it has always been done" is human nature. The semi-military structure has been perpetually transferred from police chief and sheriff with little question as to its suitability or effectiveness. An assortment of additional problems are related to the semi-military structure.

1. Police officers tend to be looked upon as having equal qualifications and abilities. Little emphasis is given to identifying the distinctive skills and abilities of individual officers.
2. The tendency for police officers to perform tasks which may be accomplished equally well by civilians is encouraged.
3. Officers are often denied the liberty of discretion and decision making that other careers allow. This may lead to a demoralizing and cynical attitude.

4. It does not promote individual initiative, innovative thinking, productivity or a sincerity to perform to the utmost of one's ability.
5. A police organization is supervised so rigidly that it's difficult for police officers to view their community without a mildly distorted frame of mind. The tendency is to perceive others in the same rigidly controlled tendency they must conform to.
6. Constructive evaluation and criticism of one's own actions is not encouraged. This hampers the personal growth and innovative thinking of individual officers. Officers must feel comfortable to challenge themselves to strive for new achievements without fearing failure.
7. The extent of an agency's uniformity and rigid structure causes many highly qualified and competent applicants selecting not to pursue a law enforcement career.
8. The limited nature of freedom for individual decision making and the lack of discretion is inconsistent with a profession and hampers efforts of law enforcement to attain professionalism.[23]

BASIC PRINCIPLES OF BUREAUCRACY

Max Weber was a renowned sociologist who influenced the world by his creation of the traditional bureaucracy theory. He extensively studied the behavior of organizations and the people within them. His theory of bureaucracy is a landmark study that identified particular dimensions of structure within bureaucratic organizations.

Weber's theory of bureaucracy is probably the most extensively discussed, examined, researched, criticized and acclaimed of all theories of formal organizations. Sociologists, administrators, philosophers, psychologists, educators, political scientists, theorists and researchers have examined the bureaucracy theory at length, due to its vast impact on organizations throughout the world. The major characteristics of the bureaucracy theory are as follows:

1. **Hierarchy of Offices** — Every administrative function in an organization is noted to have a position which entails a specific set of responsibilities and rights. All individuals assigned to a particular office are responsible for the specific rules and regulations governing that position.
2. **Specialization of Tasks** — Employees are afforded the ability to become proficient in particular tasks because work within the organization is divided among various types of job positions. Specialized training is provided to further develop expertise throughout the organization.

3. **Rules and Regulations** — Behavior throughout an organization is governed by rules and regulations. Frequently, a regulations manual is provided to members of the organization.
4. **Impersonality** — Violations of the rules and regulations of the organization are handled in an impersonal and impartially applied manner. Decisions concerning infractions are based on efficient goal attainment rather than a personal or emotional basis.
5. **Written Records** — All transactions are recorded on documents that are referred to for future reference, reasons of legalities and decision making.
6. **Salaried Personnel** — The organization is comprised of full-time salaried employees who depend upon the organization for their income.
7. **Control of Resources** — Though the organization's resources may be obtained from external origins, once acquired, they are controlled by the organization's officers.[24]

When examining the preceding characteristics, police administrators can easily relate to many if not all of them. A variety of realistic and practical problems exist with contemporary police bureaucracies. The following list of criticisms reflect more than just problems with Weber's theoretical bureaucracy model. It reflects criticisms of the manner in which present police organizations are managed.

1. The value of skills, abilities and knowledge of individual officers are often overlooked or seemingly unimportant.
2. Motivation and morale are frequently low.
3. Law enforcement agencies are unnecessarily isolated from the general public due to their militaristic structure and regulations.
4. Positive interpersonal relationships and progressive, innovative thinking is not encouraged by the bureaucracy organizational style.
5. Lastly, the typical police organization usually requires that a patrolman be dependent upon a promotion for an increase in pay or status. The same regulation applies to the detective, sergeant or other type of specialist.

   When an officer is promoted, he will most likely be transferred to a different division. As a result, the years of experience and financial investment in training become of relatively little use to him, his new assignment or the agency. This is an observably inefficient manner of administering an organization. How illogical it is to train an officer until he becomes highly proficient in performing a particular skill, then promote or transfer him to a position where those skills are virtually useless to him.

It would be a far better decision to keep the right man in a particular position. His "well rounded work experience" can be developed through in-service training that deals with the responsibilities, duties and problems of different divisions of the agencies. The value of a proficient and experienced officer is much too beneficial to throw away.

ALTERNATIVES TO BUREAUCRACY

The preceding section has identified several common fallacies of current law enforcement management. Though a more extensive examination of highly effective and efficient organizations will follow, let's examine how a stagnant, lethargic agency can be transformed into a vibrant, dynamic organizational leader. One in which apathetic, or cynical officers can become enthusiastic and develop an overpowering drive to excel.

Innovation and change are current corporate world management terms that pay a big return on their investment. Law enforcement must grasp the advantages awaiting it by designing innovative internal philosophies which create a positive change in their agency. Sheriffs and chiefs of police should view innovation and change as more than buzz words from a management text. The key to achieving significant improvements in law enforcement is for those having the authority to take the initiative to commit themselves and their agency to the pursuit of excellence.

Referring to the corporate world as a role model does not infer our nation's business community is without problems. The trade deficit increases every year. We continue to purchase more from the rest of the world than our exports pay for. America's major industries such as steel and auto are losing ground not only abroad, but at home as well. Foreign manufacturers are replacing American factories and industries on a regular basis. Statistics indicate that America's rate of productivity growth from 1966 to 1976 was lower than any of the eleven top Western industrial nations.[25]

These sobering facts have been presented in general terms. When we examine the best of America's business we find several corporate mentors from which to learn. Efficient industries and corporations now realize that the most effective working systems evolve from a high level of morale — one in which employees feel good about themselves and their accomplishments, much more so than employees in a classic bureaucracy type of organization. Increased employee involvement combined with personal and career satisfaction will generate drastically improved productivity.

Understanding the benefit of reorganizing an organizational structure to yield these benefits is not an insurmountable task. The most difficult stage of change is acquiring commitment by departmental staff. The commitment must be more than merely a decision motivated by emotion. It should be accompanied by a well developed and thoroughly considered specific plan of action. Detailed goals, objectives and roles for both individual managers and the entire organization must be specified.

Further attention will be given in latter chapters of this text to how successful corporations increase productivity. In summary, the overriding common denominator among effective organizations is that they believe productivity is directly dependent upon the level of their employees' commitment, motivation and morale. An assortment of strategies is used to assist in developing employees' imagination, innovation, dedication and belief in their own abilities. Renewed enthusiasm and vigor will spiral an organization to greater productive heights. Treating employees as the organization's first priority remains the key that unlocks the doorway to quality.

THE CHIEF ADMINISTRATOR

As any chief of police knows, the chief administrator's job is difficult and complex. Most agree it is different than what they had perceived it to be prior to their appointment. An unexpected degree of frustration seems to be common. Feeling exasperated often results from local political influences, the lack of internal staff support, and the failure to have job security and difficulty in dealing with problems generated by civil service and unions.

A recent study of nearly six hundred police chiefs revealed interesting data concerning the changes in attitude which evolved during an administrator's career. Extensive interviews and observations determined that chief administrators usually pass through five distinguishable stages.

A new chief may initially experience a degree of instability within his agency's organizational structure. Though he perceives this initial period as a time of learning about the organization, others within the agency may attempt to execute internal "power plays." City officials and/ or community leaders may also take advantage of the chief's initial vulnerability by attempting to gain some type of political influence or advantage. Determination and initiative begins to be intertwined with frustration.

The second distinguishable stage occurs within a two to four year period. This stage is characterized by a variety of power struggles both internally and outside his agency. Because he has remained the chief for several years, he has learned to adapt and adjust to situational conflicts and political battles. His frustration and cynicism tends to lessen.

If the chief has remained in office between five to nine years, he has probably enjoyed some success with internal management and implementation of programs. Any controversy concerning his reign is usually not the result of a specific policy or action. His attitudes and feelings are generally positive.

Cynicism continues to decline during the fourth stage, which usually occurs during the ten to fourteen year mark. Though they may occasionally face internal and political disturbances, virtually all chiefs have established themselves by this period. Their success is typically dependent upon having developed a sound and reliable base of support. An overall feeling of comfortability prevails.

The final stage usually begins near the fifteen year mark and continues until retirement. As retirement grows near, many administrators start to phase themselves out of their position. Relationships with others both externally and within their agency improve. Generally relaxed feelings and attitudes prevail. A degree of uneasiness will begin as retirement grows very near.[26]

Irregardless of the stage or tenure, administrators run their organization with a particular style and attitude. All those with strong values must be prepared to fight inequities and injustice. An unyielding commitment to the highest standards of ethics, fairness and professionalism must be of utmost concern throughout his organization. This will be impossible if top level management does not set the example.

As repeated evidence demonstrates, the only management style which produces optimum employee productivity is that which conveys a sincere commitment to employee personal and professional development. While administrators cannot be all things to all people, they inevitably influence the performance of every employee in the organization. There are numerous ways to recognize and show appreciation for exemplary performance. A wide array of human resource development programs are now available. Most are easily implemented. The ability to praise deserving subordinates and take decisive action to correct inefficiency is crucial. This, combined with judgement which is fair and just will succeed in the long run. Successful administrators give credit farther down the line than their own offices.[27] Nothing motivates more than a sincere interest in both the professional and personal lives of fellow officers.

The majority of sheriffs and chiefs are sincere, conscientious administrators. Though law enforcement has remained substantially behind the private sector in management expertise and innovation. Many police administrators are anxiously searching for the knowledge, and skills necessary for improvement. Conscientious administrators may find themselves struggling with these management principles because they're usually forced to learn them on their own, without professional assistance.

The quicker law enforcement can disseminate effective management information to all chief administrators, the more effective police service will be. Well respected organizations like The International Association of Chiefs of Police, The Federal Bureau of Investigation, The Police Foundation and many state organizations are making great strides in offering highly competent management courses. The more standardized and centralized law enforcement becomes, the more effective training will be. Administrators have a responsibility to participate actively in developing productive standardized methods of conveying progressive management strategies.

Every sheriff and chief must decide for himself how he will participate in improving not only his organization but law enforcement as a whole. It will take courage to step ahead of others and implement new management programs. It requires a personal quality that is rare, even among leaders. The world's greatest achievers have possessed an unusual degree of wisdom and foresight. They have used these traits to step ahead of the rest of their profession to direct innovation. Such individuals also possess loyalty, dedication, sincerity, self-confidence and the courage to do what they honestly believe is right, even if it is not a popular decision.

All of the preceding terms are consistent with an inner strength. An administrator with this quality will pursue the truth whenever or wherever it leads him. He will commit himself to "standing up" for what's right and accepting nothing less from those in his organization. He does not shy away from responsibility and is not afraid to make commitments. He fully understands that merely believing in these things is not enough. He appreciates the fact that to make a difference, he must practice what he preaches on a daily basis.

Having inner strength is very important for a police administrator— much more important than it may first appear. Realistically, this quality is unique. Most of society is preoccupied with materialistic values. No matter how a police administrator views himself, he is the strongest role model in his organization. It is he who is most responsible for whether officers are inspired to seek new challenges, make the most of their abilities and work in accordance with the highest ideals in law enforcement. A chief's inner strength will spread throughout his agency. Conversely, a lack of inner strength will infiltrate all facets of his department. True professionalism can never be achieved without the prevalence of strong, courageous leadership.

LABOR RELATIONS

Most states have adopted legal provisions which permit the practice of collective bargaining within the public sector. The agency frequently serving as a labor commission is the Public Employees Relations Committee (PERC). A union can be defined as an employee organization that represents its members for bargaining purposes.

The mere reference to labor relations creates considerable uneasiness for some administrators. The mention of police unionization generates substantial heartburn for others. Controversy over the unionization of law enforcement has raged on for decades. Though more than a half of a century evolved between the famous Boston strike of 1919 and the next major police strike, unionization of police departments has had substantial success. The number of unions throughout America may be sizeable, yet, they are not compatible with professionalism. Administrators can experience one or all of the following detrimental circumstances due to unionization.

1. Routine decision making regarding such things as transfers, discipline and hiring are unfairly restricted.
2. The public does not usually perceive unions as being consistent with professionalism.
3. Perpetual demands for improved pay and working conditions will overshadow sincere efforts to improve police performance.
4. Administrators are denied the freedom to make certain independent decisions.

There are thousands of officers who disagree with the view that unions are not good for law enforcement. Their experiences have shown that unions result in betterment for themselves and fellow officers. The fallacy in this logic is that while it is true unions improve job satisfaction by improving salaries and benefits, they do little to professionalize the police.

Realistically, there is little chance unions will disappear from law enforcement. Attaining professionalism will bring improved salaries and job satisfaction throughout the nation. Though unions may be slowing professionalism, law enforcement must learn to make the best of unionism until they are no longer deemed necessary by those who believe in them.[28]

Having faith in unionism can be tempting due to the prevalence of management which does not treat employees as well as they should. When an employer decides to place a variety of matters above the good of its employees, dissatisfaction is bound to occur. Most true professions don't have unions simply because they do not need them. As law enforcement continues to strive for professionalism, salaries and benefits will increase. Surprisingly, what is frequently shown to be more important to employees than a pay raise is the way supervisors treat them. The satisfaction or dissatisfaction of employees usually depends upon the fair or unjust manner in which they are treated.

In November of 1986, the New York City Police Department experienced the "Blue Flu." The work slow down resulted from police commissioner Benjamin Ward's plan to combat corruption in the 27 thousand member police force by rotating officers among precincts. Officers became bitter at what they perceived as an assumption they were corrupt. Morale and attitudes nosedived.

Obviously the decrease in morale resulted in a decline of quality performance. Officers in New York City during November of 1986 issued 1,403 traffic tickets. During the same weekend in 1985 they wrote 11,300 traffic tickets. They also wrote 1,922 summonses during that same weekend, compared to 26,527 the preceding year. After these statistics were published in newspapers across the nation, the image of New York's finest was tainted. The "Blue Flu" is certainly not considered professional by most Americans.

COLLECTIVE BARGAINING

The debate over whether the police should be allowed to bargain collectively continues just as it did a decade ago, or will a decade from now.

Police officers not only unionize, they are more likely to do so than the general public. Though approximately 25 percent of America's work force is unionized, nearly 50 percent of all local and state public employees are. The proportion is slightly higher for local and state police officers. Thus, to claim unions don't help the cause of professionalism, yet ignore the fact so many officers are union members, would be unrealistic. Ensuring that law enforcement collective bargaining is fair and effective is the best solution for both the police and the public they serve.

Officers unionize because they believe a union will assist in obtaining improved salary and benefits. Unions are expected to represent them effectively and aggressively. Though union members' expectations may be high, some union practices, having taken hold in the private sector, cannot be transferred to law enforcement. Collective bargaining by the police is different than that within the private sector due to laws governing labor/management relations, safety of the general public, the paramilitary nature of police agencies and the financial operations of government versus corporations.[29]

Though significant differences exist, the primary reason unions flourish remains the same in all organizations: dissatisfaction with wages, benefits and how they are treated. As police administrators become more proficient in management, the need for unionism will decrease. Organized labor is usually not sought by employees who are treated well by their immediate supervisors. While this is offensive to some, the fact remains that unions prevail where employees are supervised unfairly.

While there is no way to ensure organized labor difficulties won't occur, the possibility can be minimized by following certain guidelines.

1. Law enforcement administrators should be active in the entire labor relation process.
2. Labor relations policies designed to promote good faith and trust between the administration and union should be developed.
3. Administrators should always remain open to furthering relationships with union and government officials.
4. Administrators must accept the fact that employees have the right to form and be represented by a labor organization.
5. Administrators should make a constant effort to identify and correct areas employees have determined to be a cause of dissatisfaction.
6. Personnel benefits and working conditions must become the highest managerial priority of the organization.

7. Effective personnel leadership and management training should be conducted on a regular basis.

TRAINING AND EDUCATION

An influx of excessive funding was possible by the law enforcement assistance administration and the law enforcement educational program during the 1960's. In the 1970's, training and education prospered. Now that those funding resources are virtually non-existent, a continued effort for the development of training and education during the 80's and 90's is more necessary than ever.

LEAA funding spurred an enormous growth in the number of law enforcement courses offered by local colleges and universities. These, however, proved to be "short lived," following the elimination of federal funds. Most agencies came to expect the luxury of universities providing needed training programs. These departments were caught off guard when they were terminated. Now there is danger of a return to mediocre in-service training and a declining educational level.

One crucial element setting professions apart from occupations is that they establish and perpetuate high standards of training and education. Currently, the onset of high technology has caused a wide variety of training gimmicks to be marketed. Training gimmicks tend to gain considerable attention, yet, soon lose their appeal if patrol officers lack the basic skills necessary to do an effective job. Training must be directed toward the needs of officers "on the street."

The advancement of higher education will produce more effective and qualified police officers. At the same time, many aspects of future technology will yield tremendous benefits. As important as these areas are, it's merely human nature to direct our efforts toward interesting subjects and subconsciously ignore those less appealing.

Some of the issues contemporary law enforcement cannot continue to ignore include:

1. Increasing the supervisory ability of staff members.
2. Improving basic english skills of officers who are poor in report writing.
3. Providing improved and more frequent police driving training.
4. Law enforcement alcoholism and drug addiction.
5. Police officer mental health and suicide.

Establishing sound training priorities are crucial. Yet, most administrators find the training function a complicated issue. Concerns of civil litigation, mandatory training requirements, overtime funding restrictions and manpower shortages place most departments in a training dilemma. Irregardless of the training topic, police agencies have historically viewed in-service training in terms of the number of hours per course. Officers have been scheduled to attend classroom lectures for a particular number of hours. More often than not, lesson plans, pretests and posttests were not conducted.

The traditional in-service training model meets with varied success. The most frequent reasons why current law enforcement training programs fail include:

1. The failure of the chief administrator to provide his total support and involvement.
2. The failure to conduct a series of programs that re-enforce the agency's overall goals and objectives.
3. Failure to develop training programs which "tell it like it is."
4. The failure to simulate realism to the fullest extent possible.
5. The failure to transform theoretical knowledge into practical terms.
6. Failure to allow officers being trained to voice their opinions concerning vital issues.
7. The failure to train those who need it the most.
8. The failure to account for differences in learning abilities and levels among officers.
9. The failure to identify and utilize an agency's internal training resources efficiently.[30]

LEGAL CONSIDERATIONS

Law enforcement agencies across the nation have seen a dramatic rise in the frequency of civil litigation directed toward them. In addition to an increased number of suits, the magnitude of damage awards has become staggering. Judgements in excess of a million dollars are no longer rare.

Though not usually considered, the current state of affairs has both negative and positive repercussions. Litigation against a municipal or county government can be financially devastating. Officers directly involved in the claim may find their careers ruined. Chief administrators can be held accountable not only for an officer's specific actions, but their internal policies, regulations and training procedures as well.

Conversely, civil suits and related actions have been a tremendous, positive force in upgrading the procedures, policies and training methods of many agencies. Litigation has required many administrators to reevaluate training priorities, review departmental policies and reconsider alternatives of improvement.

There is no evidence to suggest the frequency or degree of litigation directed toward law enforcement will lessen in future years. The main areas of liability remain as follows:

1. Negligent appointment
2. Negligent retention
3. Negligent assignment
4. Negligent intrustment
5. Failure to train
6. Failure to supervise
7. Failure to direct

An extensive study conducted by American's for Effective Law Enforcement, Incorporated, during a five year period in the 1970's provides insight concerning the type and frequency of suits filed.

TYPE OF CIVIL LITIGATION	TOTAL NUMBER PER 100 OFFICERS
False arrest and prosecution	2.05%
Excessive force	2.01
Motor vehicle injuries	1.15
Miscellaneous	.94
Property damage	.69
Unknown allegations	.64
Legal search and seizure	.23
Injunctive relief	.23
Firearms related/injury caused	.22
Firearms related/death caused	.22
Liable and slander	.14
Invasion of privacy	.11[31]

The accepted standards of care demanded by civil courts continue to evolve just as does the proficiency and effectiveness of law enforcement. Administrators must remember that proper development of policy and subsequent implementation through training and supervision is crucial to minimizing liability. The National Law Enforcement Accreditation Program has begun to assist in the development and implementation of proper policies and procedures. Directly related, yet often neglected, is a thorough and effective documentation system. Detailed records in all areas of liability should be thorough and readily accessible.

Recently, an increasing number of administrators and supervisors have been found liable for the actions of subordinates when demonstrated that the administrators were negligent in their employment, supervision or training. The doctrine of sovereign immunity has historically shielded a governmental body from liability. This protection has been eroded greatly by recent legislation. Though there is still protection for governments, a 1983 U.S. Supreme Court decision partially exposed local government bodies to liabilities where the concerned injury resulted from a policy, regulation, ordinance or custom.

TECHNOLOGY

The rapid pace of today's society is being met with innovative and progressive technology. As an example, in some law enforcement agencies across the country, incoming calls are immediately analyzed by a computer which decides if and what type patrol response is appropriate. The computer instantly analyzes what patrol vehicle is available to be dispatched. Computers analyze daily crime and patrol activities, then make decisions concerning future uniform deployment.

We live in an information based society. Technology continues to develop at an incredible rate. The birth of today's technological advancements began in 1968 with passing of the Omnibus Crime Control and Safe Streets Act. It, in turn, resulted in the creation of the Law Enforcement Assistance Administration. The availability of funding from LEAA for technological research and development seemed virtually endless during the 1970's.

Lazer technology, computerized latent fingerprint searching, highly sophisticated communication systems, greatly improved special weapons and tactics equipment, forensic science improvements, video training technology and sophisticated surveillance devices are currently available to the police. The amount of benefit derived from state of the art technology will largely depend upon the initiative of those within each agency. Administrators must be willing to commit the manpower necessary to adequately investigate, develop and implement new technology based programs. Thorough research and development should be conducted prior to every financial commitment. More than one department has been guilty of literally "throwing money away" for what was later to be considered a worthless gimmick. The advance of police telecommunications is another clear example of how technological advancements have been a tremendous benefit. Initially, teletypes were transmitted only by wire through the American Telegraph and Telephone Company. Future evolutions included the use of telephone lines for law enforcement, paper tape documentation and independent state regulations. The law enforcement telecommunications service (LETS) was created to combat the high expense of communicating across state lines. Following an extended overloading of transmissions, LETS was upgraded in 1976. It is now known as the National Law Enforcement Telecommunication Service (NLETS). This highly sophisticated and computerized transmission service currently provides communications for all fifty states and Canada.

Though communication systems of today are far advanced from those of decades ago, our technological victory is a shallow one. Computerized communication systems do allow most officers to be equipped with portable communication no matter what their location. Mechanically operated teletype machines are almost obsolete. They will probably be phased out within the next few years and be replaced with computerized systems. The communications advancement remain a shallow success because even this vastly improved speed is not quick enough. Wanted criminals are set free daily because "wanted checks" are not relayed to the requesting officer rapidly enough.

Computerized advancements like those in the communication areas are not achieved without a high price. Finances often prohibit small agencies from computerizing record systems, communication sections, driver's license histories and vehicle registrations. As the need for an information based society is acknowledged by the public, increased funding will be allotted. In addition, the expense of such technology should decrease in the near future.[32]

Assessing the cost of advanced technology as unaffordable is frequently superficial logic. Not only does advanced technology increase the effectiveness of performed tasks, it will enhance the ability and potential of officers themselves. Officers making $10 an hour have an annual salary of approximately $20,000. This is a sizable investment. Salaries are usually the single greatest expense of any agency. Computer assisted instruction and interactive video training can increase training comprehension and retention considerably. Technology will develop officers who are more efficient and effective. Thus, the greatest return on the original salary investment is only achieved with quality improvement.

From a budgetary perspective, substantial funds can be saved due to a decrease in overtime because this form of training can be conducted on duty. The savings will easily pay for the expense of purchasing "state of the art" equipment. Interactive video and computer assisted instruction systems are of tremendous assistance for manpower problems as well. Officers will be able to participate in effective training at their own pace, without the necessity of taking groups of officers away from their regular duties, as with classroom instruction. Programs can be implemented so they simply log their training into a computer and participate in as many lessons as time permits. If required to leave, they may begin again, where they left off.

The amount of time required by officers for a particular training program will only be a matter of how quickly they are able to learn the material. They are not dependent upon the rate others are going. All programs are automatically standardized both in terms of documentation and quality of material. The age old problem of training versus manpower can be remedied since a computer and video system are available 24 hours a day, 7 days a week. Little strain on manpower is created when officers can come off the street one at a time.

Chief administrators must be committed to at least investigate the feasibility of training technology available both today and in the future. This movement should be the result of a determined commitment based on systematic long range plans that will continue to meet the needs of a progressive agency. There is no question technology can improve the effectiveness and efficiency of the American system of law enforcement. The obstacle is the hesitancy of sheriffs and police chiefs to devote themselves and their agencies to the change required.

LAW ENFORCEMENT PLANNING

The scope, purpose and benefits of planning have been described in numerous ways by a variety of people. The process has been both criticized and complimented. Those who tend to belittle the need for planning most likely do not appreciate its benefits or potential. Those with this view probably practice "management by crisis" on a regular basis. They don't view planning as important for sound management. The internal functions of their organizations tend to respond to events, as opposed to anticipating and shaping them.

Planning may be looked upon as an agency's decision making process for the future. Yet, it is a great deal more than simply forecasting the future. Planning provides administrators with guidelines to improve the future of his organization. Additional benefits include:

1. Provides agencies with a clear mission or purpose.
2. Encourages an improved commitment and responsibility from employees.
3. Encourages more efficient use of resources.
4. Improves harmony and cooperation among divisions within the department.
5. Provides substantial justification for funding requests.
6. Assists in clarifying goals and objectives.
7. An essential ingredient for maintaining optimum efficiency and effectiveness of the organization.
8. Improves the analysis of problems and methods for problem solving.
9. It is consistent with attaining a standard of professionalism.
10. Instills a sense of pride and accomplishment throughout the agency.

Although not the present situation, every law enforcement agency should develop and use an established planning process. Obviously, smaller agencies will be forced to use officers with additional responsibilities. The magnitude and complexity of planning projects will frequently be affected by the size of the agency. Irregardless of size, most police organizations that have established a planning process use a traditional planning model. The model involves a systematic, step-by-step process.

Step 1 — Commitment and preparation for the planning project.
Step 2 — Description of the present situation.
Step 3 — Develop projections.
Step 4 — Consider the anticipated future status of concerned variables.
Step 5 — Identify problems.
Step 6 — Establish goals.
Step 7 — Identify alternative courses of action.
Step 8 — Select preferred alternatives.
Step 9 — Plan for implementation.
Step 10 — Implement plans.
Step 11 — Monitor and evaluate progress.[33]

Unfortunately, most departments haven't developed an effective planning procedure. The traditional procedures require many steps be based upon a sound collection of statistics and data. Therefore, accurate projections and productive planning requires that agencies have a reliable record keeping and data analysis procedure. Failing to do so renders many planning efforts unreliable.

In the past, apathy, convenience and tradition were often substituted for proper analysis. Less than 1 percent of all funding for the American Criminal Justice System has been spent on research. As a result, the most effective ways to prevent, detect, apprehend or prosecute criminals may not have been determined. As with many agencies, the entire judicial system has generally floated without a strong sense of direction or established priorities.[34]

Some administrators don't have an organized planning process because they believe their agency cannot afford the additional workload. In reality, these agencies can't afford to be without a formal planning process. Other administrators mistakenly believe planning is too theoretical and provides few practical benefits. Typical planning assignments include evaluating current and proposed internal programs, analyzing and predicting internal productivity, assisting budget justification and preparation, assisting the planning of tactical operations, testing, recommending or disapproving the purchase of various equipment and assuming responsibility for the preparation of proposals having to do with various innovative programs.

Law enforcement agencies which establish an effective, continual planning process will be more productive than those without it. There's a variety of distinctive types of plans. Tactical plans involve planning for specific situations at anticipated locations. Procedural plans are ordinarily included within an agency's written directive system. Operational plans are developed for services within an organization. Managerial plans involve the formation of purpose, goals and policies. They determine the responsibilities, authority and structure of an organization.

Irregardless of the type, all effective plans will have certain characteristics:

1. Plans should be flexible enough to allow for unforseen developments.
2. Plans must be specific enough to be easily understood and reduce the potential for misunderstandings.
3. Plans must be based upon a sound foundation of thorough research and development.
4. Plans must provide considerable emphasis on the long range results of immediate actions.
5. Coordination with other agencies and governments must be considered.
6. As many employees as practical should participate in the developing of plans.[35]

CONCLUSIONS

This chapter has concentrated on law enforcement's "state of the art" and what actions may increase efficiency, productivity and professionalism. Certainly, deficient areas exist. The judicial system is a reflection of society. As society changes, so will the criminal justice process.

When all perspectives are considered, those who have chosen law enforcement as their life's work have great reason to be proud. The purpose of this book is not to accent the accomplishments of the police, though there are many. Instead, the book's focus has been on the making of professionalism. No one should "make light of" or diminish our past achievements. Law enforcement has improved more in the last two decades than it had in the last century. Dedication, hard work and loyalty to the highest ideals and standards exist in every law enforcement agency in America.

While sincerity and hard work are necessary ingredients for professionalism, future efforts must be more standardized and consistent with effective managerial strategies. The advent of a nationwide accreditation process will greatly expedite professionalism. It's virtually impossible for a chief administrator to substantially improve his organization if he doesn't have specific standards to strive for. Accreditations' high standards, combined with nationwide standardization is serving as a catalyst for professionalism.

Every administrator should support and encourage the spread of accreditation. As professionalism grows, resistance based upon philosophies inconsistent with professionalism will diminish. Professionalism may eventually eliminate the need for civil service, unionism and the semi-paramilitary organizational structure. In doing so, police officers will be better paid, more respected, have greater self-esteem and feel as though the organization they work for really cares about them.

REFERENCES

1. Richard H. Ward, "Policing The World, An International Perspective," *Law and Order,* April 1986, pg. 20-22.
2. Richard H. Ward, "Policing The World, An International Perspective," *Law and Order,* April 1986, pg. 21-22.
3. Walter L. Ames, *Police and Community In Japan,* University of California Press, Berkeley, California, 1981, pg. 214.

4. George Korzeniowski, The Royal Canadian Mounted Police, *Law and Order,* April 1986, pg. 40-42.

5. David H. Bayly, *Forces of Order — Police Behavior In Japan and the United States,* University of California Press, Berkeley, California, 1976, pg. 184-187.

6. Walter L. Ames, *Police and Community In Japan,* University of California Press, Berkeley, California, 1981, pg. 12-14.

7. David H. Bayley, *Forces of Order — Police Behavior In Japan and the United States,* University of California Press, Berkeley, California, 1976, pg. 189-191.

8. David H. Bayley, *Forces of Order — Police Behavior In Japan and the United States,* University of California Press, Berkeley, California, 1976, pg. 184-194.

9. James Q. Wilson, *Varieties of Police Behavior,* Harvard University Press, Cambridge, Mass., 1968, pg. 30-31.

10. Richard H. Ward, "The Police Role: A Case of Diversity," *The Journal of Criminal Law Criminology and Police Science,* Northwestern University School of Law, Vol. 61, No. 4, pg. 211-215.

11. Roy R. Roberg, *The Changing Police Role,* Justice Systems Development, Inc., San Jose, California, 1976, pg. 88.

12. Roy R. Roberg, *The Changing Police Role,* Justice Systems Development, Inc., San Jose, California, 1976, pg. 90.

13. Delmar Karlen, *Anglo-American Criminal Justice,* Oxford University Press, New York, New York, 1967, pg. 10-11.

14. U.S. Department of Justice, *Report To The Nation On Crime and Justice,* Bureau of Justice Statistics, U.S. Government Printing Office, 1983, pg. 44.

15. O.W. Wilson and Roy Clinton McLaren, *Police Administration,* McGraw-Hill, New York, New York, 1972, pg. 246-251.

16. Charles R. Swanson and Leonard Territo, *Police Administration,* Macmillan, New York, New York, 1983, pg. 212-219.

17. Daniel J. Bell, "The Police-Personnel Upgrading For Professionalism," *The Police Chief,* Gaithersburg, MD., January 1978, pg. 32-33.

18. Charles R. Swanson and Leonard Territo, *Police Administration,* Macmillan, New York, New York, 1983, pg. 33-36.

19. Bureau of Justice Statistics, *Justice Expenditure and Employment, 1983,* U.S. Department of Justice, U.S. Government Printing Office, Wash., D.C., 1986, pg. 1.

20. Florida Highway Patrol, Tallahassee, Florida, 1986.

21. David Marc Kleinman, "In The Midwest, What's Bad For General Motors is Bad For The Police," *Police Magazine.* May, 1981, pg. 23-31.

22. Charles R. Swanson and Leonard Territo, *Police Administration,* Macmillan, New York, New York, 1983, pg. 335-338.

23. George G. Killinger and Paul F. Cromwell, Jr., *Issues In Law Enforcement,* Holbrook Press, Inc., Boston, Mass., 1975, pg. 318-322.

24. Paula F. Silver, *Educational Administration,* Harper & Row, New York, New York, 1983, pg. 74-77.

25. Francois Basili, "Work Up America," *Work Dynamics,* Paramus, N.J., October 1986, pg. 6.

26. John P. Crank, Robert M. Regoli, Eric D. Poole, Robert G. Culbertson, "Cynicism Among Police Chiefs," *Justice Quarterly,* Washington, D.C., September 1986, pg. 343-347.

27. Schuyler Meyer, "Personal Rewards Are the Mainstay of the Police Chief's Job," *The Police Chief,* March 1986, pg. 18-23.

28. Richard M. Ayres, "Police Unions: A Step Toward Professionalism?," *Journal of Police Science and Administration,* Northwestern University School of Law, Vol. 3, No. 4, 1975, pg. 400-404.

29. William P. Hobgood, "Should Police Be Permitted To Organize and Bargain Collectively?," *F.B.I. Law Enforcement Bulletin,* January 1981, pg. 1-2.

30. Larry L. Lambert, "Nine Reasons Why Most Training Programs Fail," *Personnel Journal,* January 1985, pg. 62-64.

31. Americans For Effective Law Enforcement, Incorporated, *The Patrol Company Lawyer,* February-March 1980, pg. 24.

32. John Probert, "Police Telecommunications: The Influence of Computers On Law Enforcement," *The Police Chief,* May 1986, pg. 53-54.

33. Robert Cushman, *Criminal Justice Planning For Local Governments,* Washington, D.C., U.S. Government Printing Office, 1980, pg. 26.

34. Alvin W. Cohn, *Criminal Justice Planning and Development,* Sage Publications, Beverly Hills, California 1977, pg. 22-26.

35. Charles R. Swanson and Leonard Territo, *Police Administration,* Macmillan, New York, New York, 1983, pg. 386-410.

Chapter 4

LEARNING FROM THE CORPORATE WORLD

Law ENFORCEMENT has struggled toward professionalism for more than half a century. Tremendous effort by a relatively small group of individuals and organizations has resulted in great advancements during the last two decades. Irregardless of how much funding is appropriated, technological advances alone, cannot lead to professionalism; neither can improved patrol procedures or investigative advancements. Enhanced crime prevention, training and higher educational levels will not succeed by themselves.

The single most important factor in reaching professionalism is improved leadership. This doesn't mean the chief administrators of the forty thousand law enforcement agencies across the nation have not done a good job. Everything considered, management has done their best with the knowledge and tools afforded them. As with all endeavors, however, increased knowledge will lead to improved abilities and better leadership.

Unfortunately, law enforcement's managerial expertise has lagged behind the quality of leadership in the business community. There is no reason why this must continue. A more aggressive, innovative philosophy can make the difference between mediocrity and the quality of performance the police need in the future. Once again, the administrators must make the difference.

The future of police partially depends on whether sheriffs and chiefs truly appreciate how much difference they can make. The combined forces of positive thinking, determination and enlightened leadership can make the dream of professionalism become reality.

CORPORATE LEADERSHIP HISTORY

Effective management has always been of concern to societies. Egyptian records dating as far back as 1300 B.C. indicate their recognition

79

of administration and organization. Confucius' writings in China made reference to strategies for proper public management. The success of the Roman Empire is largely credited to the Roman's ability to manage and organize. Lastly, Socrates' records of early Greece document remarkably skillfull management expertise.

One of the most efficient formal organizations throughout the history of Western Civilization has been the Roman Catholic church. The effectiveness of its managerial techniques and organizational strategies have had a great deal to do with its centuries of existence. The specialization of activities consistent with functional lines, a hierachy of authority and the use of staff are examples of their managerial skill.[1]

Whether we reflect upon leaders such as Julius Caesar and Moses or more contemporary counterparts, common denominators seem to appear. Irregardless of the era or type of organization, all great leaders possessed an incredible sincerity for their purpose, were very hard workers and had strong personal character. These same leaders, however, may disagree on fundamental management techniques and principles. As with most matters, time has a way of refining beliefs once thought to be the most effective, but now know to be flawed.

During one period in history, leaders were thought to be born, not made. The so called "great man" theory was based upon the premise that inheritance and breeding determined the identity of future leadership. This belief held that no degree of learning or ability could change an individual's fate.

When this theory failed to adequately explain how or why people become leaders, it was replaced by the view that great events created leaders from otherwise ordinary individuals. Believers felt that Lenin was simply "minding his own business" when a revolution began around him. The inadequacies of such logic were soon apparent and this theory was also dismissed.

The preceding theories have come and gone because they could not stand the test of time. They, like others, failed to account for an assortment of practical aspects of management and leadership.[2] Historically, the study of leaders and leadership has followed a continuous evolutionary cycle. Whether military, religious or business, all organizations and leaders have sought self-improvement.

In America, the "modern" industrial system took shape between 1890 and 1920. Frederick W. Taylor is generally referred to as the founder of modern scientific management. His famous text, *The Principles of Scientific Management* was published in 1911. The book held that America was riddled with inefficiency and its remedy could be found in systematic management rather than an extraordinary individual. Furthermore, Taylor professed effective management is a true science, based upon distinctive rules, laws and principles. These principles are applicable to all kinds of human activities. When properly applied, proponents felt astounding improvements will follow.

The 1930's was a period when the business world was forced to critically analyze their methods of operation. The Great Depression and an upswing in unionism were directing national focus upon the failures of industrial management. Business administrators and managers were, often for the first time, being held accountable for their actions.

Further concentration on management was generated by the outbreak of the 2nd World War. Emphasis was directed toward increased production with the least possible use of manpower and materials. Managerial know how became crucial as the urgency to produce efficiently and quickly was paramount.

Many commonly accepted principles of supervision originated from military organizations. Few organizations in the history of Western Civilization have been forced to manage such large groups. A rigid chain of command relationship, adherence to strict discipline, staff functions and emphasis on training earmark military administration. Many of these principles are still used by civilian organizations. Law enforcement is a prime example of the military managerial transference.

With World War II as its catalyst, the 1950's experienced a movement toward more refined business skills. When military leaders pursued civilian careers, many militaristic supervisory practices were transmitted to free enterprise. As the size of industries increased, effective management became more complex. Additional skilled and proficient managers were needed. American industry was well on its way to world dominance. Spurred on by the principles of "scientific management," America's corporate world entered a decade when it was recognized as the most effective, productive, economic force on earth.[3]

The 1960's marked the beginning of a dramatic business transformation era. During the next two decades the world dominance of American industry, which had been enjoyed and taken for granted, began to crumble. Foreign countries established a foothold on vital supplies of raw materials. Foreign competition which had never been taken seriously was now threatening many of our major industries.

One glaring example of the threat from foreign trade was in the sale of Japanese automobiles within America. From 1960 to 1980, sales skyrocketed from 1 1/4 of 1 percent to a whomping 22 percent of the market. Consumer prices nearly tripled during the same time period, rising almost 180 percent. The United States also lost 23 percent of its share of World Markets during the 1970's, according to U.S. Commerce Department of Statistics.[4]

Additional evidence of America's economic decline was apparent. By the summer of 1982, business failures had risen to the highest level they had been for half a century. Innovation declined as the rate of inventions decreased substantially during the last few decades. These and other problem areas were perpetuated by the fact we had simply come to take our business dominance for granted. As with all endeavors, self-serving assumptions frequently increase the probability of losing any achievements which have been accomplished.[5]

Numerous influences within society have changed the way we view organizations. Consumer activists, civil liberty unions, minority rights organizations, political causes, labor organizations and an assortment of protest movements have and continue to alter our opinions. America has experienced enormous social changes during the last two decades. In summary:

- Many collective bargaining agreements now contain provisions requiring management/labor committees to solve special production difficulties.
- The number of employees having flexible working hours has grown to approximately 10 percent. Unions now bargain for reduced work weeks.
- More than half of all families have at least two employed individuals.
- Most wives are now employed.
- Both employer contributions and benefits of employee health coverage have increased.
- The median level of formal education for the entire labor force has increased to more than one year of college. State and federal legislation was passed which barred employment discrimination.[6]

Evolution and revolution were trademarks of the 1960-1980 era. After losing great strides in corporate dominance, the business community began to investigate remedies for its ills. Some organizations started to move beyond traditional management and address the barriers to creativity. They provided employees with the skills and techniques to overcome the negativism of previous management styles.

Nationwide corporate evolution was occurring as progressive businesses recognized the need for an organizational climate that fostered new approaches and ideas. These were organizations which stimulated and managed innovation. They focused on the development of human resources. Methods to successfully implement progressiveness was viewed as a critical ingredient to success.

JAPANESE MANAGEMENT

There have been a variety of articles and books in recent years regarding Japanese business methodology. Most of this notoriety has been positive; and justifiably so. Japan is a nation of 110 million people who occupy only 1/4 of 1 percent of the world's land, yet, produce 1/10 of the world's gross national product. The secret to their success is the efficiency, organization and development of human resources.[7]

Employment Procedures — Though the majority of smaller businesses practice employment procedures fairly similar to those in the United States, the top 40 percent of Japanese corporations usually hire their personnel for life. The business makes a commitment to provide extensive training based on job rotation. The employee makes a commitment to work for the employer until he retires. Most employees are transferred from one division to another every several years. Having all employees participate in job rotations develops more knowledgeable and understanding employees.

Those hired by Japanese corporations rarely have unique specialties. Corporations would rather hire applicants with adequate potential, but relatively unskilled. This allows effective human resource development strategies to mold new employees in the manner most productive to the business.

Promotion System — Unlike the United States, promotions are based on more than performance and ability — commitment, interpersonal relationships, loyalty to the organization and co-workers, courtesy and cooperation are strongly considered. The ability for all employees to work in harmony for the good of the organization is emphasized and encouraged whenever possible.

Career advancement is generally much slower than in the United States. This is accepted and understood long before the employee is hired. Frequently, employees who begin their careers on the same date are promoted as a group. They receive improved benefits and salaries of equal amounts. Once again, little or no resentment is experienced. Psychological rewards like subtle recognition or increased responsibility are frequently provided in lieu of financial gain.[8]

Managerial philosophy is a fundamental reason for the effectiveness of Japanese business. Evidence indicates a major difference between the American management style and that of Japan is that we have remained set in old, hard fast perceptions and beliefs. If American law enforcement is to make substantial betterments, they too must break away from traditional management molds.

Examining the effectiveness of the Japanese will assist in learning to motivate employees, organize and delegate efficiently and to develop human resources. Because improved management is the key to the overall quality of an organization, it is demonstrated repeatedly in Japanese companies. Society's best run corporations are convinced their ability to compete in the open market depends on their success at inspiring employees to strive for productivity, instead of becoming stagnant, apathetic and indifferent.

Management Style — The Japanese culture places tremendous emphasis on tradition and heritage. This greatly affects the management and leadership style of an employment setting. The skills used by management to develop human resources are passed on to successors. An attitude quite different than that in America prevails. Strong human resource management and quality improvement has greatly increased their productivity.

The majority of Japanese managers view their employees as individuals to be honored in achieving the organization's purposes. Compare this to leaders who see employees only as objects for their own end. Interdependent management provides significant organizational advantages. Just as the Japanese culture encourages administrators to be interdependent, it also produces supervisors who convey sincerity, caring and understanding toward employees.

Japanese management, however, is similar to that of the United States in organizational structure and systems. The substantial difference remains in management skills, goals and style. People, not equipment, money or profit are considered Japan's main resource. Their "people" approach ultimately enhances efficiency and productivity. The final result is increased profit.

The quality of employee performance evolves around the employee being motivated. If management really is not concerned with employees, little motivation or sincerity will exist. The Japanese believe an effective organization relies on the innovation and creativity of its employees. Instilling the feeling of being needed and demonstrating that an employee's opinion matters, fertilizes the growth of increased performance. When the relationship between an administrator and employee is based on loyalty, respect and commitment, a successful organization is usually ensured.[9]

TOKYO LAW ENFORCEMENT

Metropolitan Tokyo, like all local police organizations, is part of a national police force controlled by the National Public Safety Commission and its subordinate, National Police Agency. Prior to the end of the second World War, Japanese police operated under a centralized system.

During the post war era, a law was enacted to change the centralized police system to a decentralized system — one similar to that used in the United States and England. The 1947 legislation brought law enforcement procedures more in line with the allied forces then occupying the country. All cities having a population in excess of 5,000 citizens would maintain their own police force. In addition, for the first time in Japan, a democratic method of administering law enforcement was established.

Though these changes provided more democracy, the efficiency and effectiveness of Japan's police force was clearly reduced. Smaller communities found less efficient police services with a vastly increased financial burden. Within a few years, enough pressure had developed to revise the decentralized policies.

In June of 1954, a new law was adopted to combine the concepts of centralization and democracy into the police structure. Still in effect today, highlights of the system include a democratic administration and political neutrality. One unified police service was again established throughout the country. The financial burden imposed on smaller municipalities was lessened. Japan had found a way to meet the needs of the country, yet remain flexible and responsive. Their law enforcement remains under the control of The National Commission and its administrative branch, The National Police Agency. The prime minister provides leadership to the National Commission.[10]

Japan has developed one of the most effective, if not the most effective, methods of crime control in the world. Using Tokyo as an example, it is apparent many similarities can be drawn between cities in Japan and America. Tokyo is a city of approximately 12 million people living within 800 square miles. This ratio is similar to that of many major American cities. The ratio of police to population is also fairly similar. Tokyo has a ratio of one officer to every 270 citizens. Several large

American cities have a higher officer/citizen ratio. The Tokyo crime rate, on the other hand, is much lower than that of comparable American municipalities. Of the crimes committed in Japan, violent crimes comprise less than 20 percent.

What makes Tokyo successful at controlling crime? One obvious reason is that the Japanese have a less violent society than the United States. This is certainly a substantial influence, but additional differences exist. Differences which America would be wise to consider adapting:

1. Centralization of one unified police force provides superior effectiveness and efficiency.
2. An organizational climate that promotes both personal and career development. A management style which treats employees as their top priority.
3. The Tokyo Metropolitan Police Department places an extreme emphasis upon establishing and maintaining close community contact with citizens. Approximately 100 separate police stations exist within the metropolitan area.
4. Police education and training receives greater significance in Tokyo than in America. Recruiting college graduates is always emphasized. Basic training at the Metropolitan training school lasts for a year. College graduates are only required to attend for six months. After one year's service, officers return to the school for an additional six weeks of training. Centralization allows all training to be totally standardized.[11]

Current Japanese Trends — Japanese management is known for its seniority based promotion system and lifetime employment. Employees are characterized as diligent, dedicated and sincere. Seemingly endless improvements originate and are proposed by frontline workers. Teamwork and cooperation are embraced as the resources that produce optimum efficiency and productivity.

Just as America's best industries, Japan is known for its continual effort for self-improvement. Undaunted by the fear of failure, the best managed corporations constantly try new ideas in the pursuit of excellence. Some of the current Japanese business trends include:

1. **Accommodating Work Hours** — Increased attempts to accommodate employee's preferred work hours are prevalent throughout Japan. Employers find that increasing the length of shifts and attempting to accommodate the hours employees request to work are deriving benefits. Positive changes in work schedules produce happier employees who show their appreciation by sincerity and hard work.

2. **Use of Computers** — The hidden qualities and abilities of employees are now compiled in computer systems. Continued emphasis on human resource development has established computerized "skill inventories" to reference particular abilities and skills.

3. **Decreased Work Week** — The standard Japanese work week is eight hours a day, six days a week. Some are now proposing to reduce this tradition to a statutory nine-hour, five-day plan. Irregardless of the pending change, the Japanese remain true, hard working people. Only 57.6 percent take the vacation days coming to them.

4. **Wellness Programs** — Contrary to the opinion many Americans may have of Japanese industry, health and fitness programs have not played an intrical part of Japanese industry. Corporations have frequently done only enough to satisfy national labor laws. An assortment of wellness programs are now being implemented at an ever increasing frequency.

5. **Meditation Rooms and Culture Courses** — Japanese meditation rooms are relatively small rooms, usually containing only a chair and desk. Their purpose is to furnish a quiet spot for any employee to think or meditate without distraction. Culture courses are offered by management to encourage harmony and friendliness among employees. All levels of employees attend courses such as music, art, cooking or horticulture.[12]

In summary, the wisdom to be learned from examining Japanese management is similar to what America's best corporations now know. While cultural differences exist, both worlds derive success from establishing a managerial philosophy that promotes its employees as their highest priority. An atmosphere of caring, sincerity and inspiration prevails in efficient organizations. For any organization to remain productive over an extended period of time, its members must truly enjoy their work. Management can make the difference.

QUALITY CIRCLES

The use of quality circles is a management technique commonly thought to have been borrowed from the Japanese. While some management experts contend circles were used in America far before the Japanese influence was felt, they've been successful in Japan for a long time.

Following World War II, scores of American soldiers spread throughout the nation starting all types of businesses. Industries grew at astounding rates. As expected, all levels of supervisors molded themselves after the military style of management — bureaucracy/strict authoritarian. Before long, prior military supervisors were assuming management positions throughout the nation. Sometimes, the only way they knew to supervise was through fear and intimidation.

In contrast to this bureaucratic/authoritarian and sometimes dictatorship style, a few quality control experts professed the opposite form of management, following the second World War. Their message was employee participation instead of employer dictatorship. Treating employees with respect and dignity in lieu of viewing them as merely machines and sound statistical analysis instead of guessing. After finding criticism and ridicule in America, they went to Japan. The response was phenomenal. The Japanese embraced them with open arms. The result is now well known.

The basic premise of quality control circles is that employees who actually do a task are best suited to investigate the possible improvements regarding it. Involving employees generates more incentive to work with initiative and dedication. Employee motivation is heightened when there is direct involvement in a managerial decision making process. Management still makes the final decision. Quality circles act as "fact finders."

The Champaign, Illinois Police Department have found their quality circle process to be a productive tool. These were their implementation steps.

Step 1 — Determine how and when the quality circle will meet. The Champaign Police Department reorganized their patrol shifts to provide for a common training day each week. The quality circle program used half of the training day for their meeting.

Step 2 — Determine topics for discussion during the first quality control circle meeting. Some of the topics developed in Champaign included improving radio procedures, D.U.I. Enforcement, the prostitution problem and changing departmental forms.

Step 3 — Supervisors throughout the department must thoroughly explain the quality circle concept to all subordinates. The goals, objectives and benefits must be stressed to prevent misunderstandings or resistance so common with the implementation of a new program.[13]

Generally, quality circles are groups of six to ten employees who meet to identify problems and determine practical solutions. Though most quality circles produce very positive results, Thomas Peters and Robert Waterman, authors of the highly acclaimed *In Search of Excellence* are quick to issue a warning. "The current gimmick is the quality circle.

There is absolutely nothing wrong with the idea, as the Japanese have so forcefully reminded us. The quality circles are only the latest in a long line of tools that can either be very helpful, or can simply serve as a smoke screen while management continues to get away with not doing its job of real people management."

The Japanese began quality circles in 1962. By 1984, there were over 192,000. Some Americans try to emanate the Japanese success without having the supportive culture so important in Japan. America began implementing quality circles in the late 1970's. By 1981, approximately 2,500 quality circles were operating in the United States. In 1982, a survey by the New York Stock Exchange indicated 44 percent of all companies with more than 500 employees had quality circles. Experts now estimate over 90 percent of the Fortune 500 companies have used quality circles.[14]

Recently, however, a small portion of the American corporate world has become somewhat disenchanted with the concepts of quality circles. What had been heralded as the solution to unproductiveness is now occasionally referred to as a technique that isn't quite worth the effort. The negative views include allegations such as:

1. They won't work in America because American workers aren't as dedicated or docile as Japanese workers.
2. They have limited applications.
3. Top level management fails to make a true commitment to the quality circle concept.
4. Quality circles can't document dollar and cents savings.
5. Many industries haven't taught the same quality circle techniques the Japanese taught.

It is not true that a substantial portion of American corporations have disbanded their quality circles. What is true is that many corporations have changed the form of their quality circles. Others have begun calling them by a different term. There seems to be a second generation of the quality circle movement in America. To an extent, it's very similar to the first movement, except it appears to enjoy even greater acceptance and operate on a much wider scope within the company. Instead of identifying only particular problems, America's new quality circles are more concerned with company-wide quality management.

The latest belief is that original quality circle management did not achieve total involvement of employees. Contemporary quality improvement is moving toward organization-wide participation and involvement. Many companies have found it necessary to restructure internal organizations before a total employee involvement is experienced.

In summary, quality circles have weathered the test of time to take a place among the most effective proven management strategies. Most of those who remain skeptical probably do not appreciate the depth of involvement and commitment from supervision necessary for true quality improvement. Quality circles cannot be used as a smoke screen to pacify employees. Management must be sincerely committed to real people involvement. Applied without the utmost of top administrative thrust, quality circles simply will not work. Implemented with intense administrative support, they will be an extremely beneficial part of the overall formula of excellence.[15] Professional consultation will be necessary to be successful in transforming management.

THE SEARCH FOR EXCELLENCE

Every chief and sheriff has the opportunity to ensure his agency's professionalism. In doing so, he is searching for excellence. Learning of law enforcement's past, current and future struggle for professionalism may influence his personal perspective. He certainly doesn't need to wait for state or federal guidelines or other forms of assistance to pursue professionalism. The search for police excellence begins with taking one giant step; a sincere commitment.

Making the commitment may be more difficult than it appears. At first glance, most administrators believe they've already made this commitment. After all, they are dedicated, sincere and loyal to the highest ideals of the police. They attend numerous seminars and management training courses. Rational management practices and principles have been learned. Executives ensure that middle management and line supervisors attend appropriate supervision courses. Virtually all the staff is versed on the traditional fundamentals of management and supervision.

As expected, it is traditional management that generates difficulty in carrying out the commitment. Since the commitment involves restructuring the managerial philosophy of the organization, traditional principles, especially the semi-military structure, must be transformed. Remember, teamwork and people-management are the qualities that have made America's best run companies so successful. Police administrators must commit themselves and their staff to a management which develops the skills, abilities and potential within all employees of the organization.

An organization's atmosphere, managerial policies and leadership style are the real issues to be considered when it is being evaluated. As the police executive research forum stated in their publication, *How to Rate Your Local Police,* arrest rates, response times, crime rates or the percent of investigative clearances are important, but should not be the first consideration. The initial concern must focus upon administrative management style. When an agency's leadership treats employees as the organization's most important resource, matters such as crime and arrest rates will improve naturally.

MANAGERIAL PERSPECTIVE

The Japanese enjoy a tremendous advantage over the United States regarding managerial views, values and attitudes. Their managerial perspective was shaped long before they were old enough to become leaders. How much easier it would be for Americans if they had a similar unity of purpose. A unified perspective promotes cooperation and togetherness. It fosters the view that the development of human resources is a necessary ingredient for professionalism.

The Japanese business world uses their culture of togetherness and unity to its fullest advantage. New employees of large corporations begin work on the same day, April 1st. They usually start employment as a group, wear matching uniforms and receive identical salaries. Employees often sing or recite a daily song or creed. As an example, 87,000 employees of the Matsushita Electric Company sing and recite the following text at precisely 8 A.M. each day:

> **Employees Creed.** Progress and development can be realized only through the combined efforts and cooperation of each member of our company. Each of us, therefore, shall keep this idea constantly in mind as we devote ourselves to the continuous improvement of our company.
>
> **Basic Business Principles.** To recognize our responsibilities as industrialists, to foster progress, to promote the general welfare of society, and to devote ourselves to the further development of world culture.[16]

Japan's industry has encouraged the belief that a business should evolve around the good of its community. A profit margin should not be viewed from only a monetary sense. It should represent the confidence society has in the company. In Japan, the following seven spiritual values are instilled within employees as values they and the corporation must strive for:

The Seven Spiritual Values
1. National service through industry
2. Fairness
3. Harmony and cooperation
4. Struggle for betterment
5. Courtesy and humility
6. Adjustment and assimilation
7. Gratitude[17]

The managerial philosophy of the administration in the Matsushita Electric Company is exemplified through a variety of daily activities. Though the Japanese demonstrate widespread continuity of managerial purpose, shining examples of American leadership should not be overlooked. Understanding the leadership perspectives of America's best run corporation, and appreciating why they developed such views, are invaluable insights for law enforcement.

A great number of articles have been written regarding Japanese management. Teamwork to the extent of singing company songs and chanting corporate slogans are frequently dismissed as something that could not occur in the United States. Yet, American examples of exceptional management does. Mary Kay Cosmetics and Tupperware create incredible enthusiasm and excitement at festive employee meetings and rallies. During IBM sales training, workers sing songs almost every morning. Hewlett-Packard furnishes "beer busts," when appropriate, to keep workers filled with harmony and cooperation.[18]

In Search of Excellence, the highly acclaimed business text by Thomas J. Peters and Robert H. Waterman, Jr., identifies what America's truly excellent companies are doing that the rest are not. The best run companies emphasize the following eight ingredients of a successful management recipe.

1. **They prefer to act** rather than waste time undergoing cycles of analysis and debate. Planning and research are admirable, yet a decision must be made and action must follow.
2. They appreciate the value of **staying close to their customer.** Understanding his needs and preferences are crucial to success.
3. They **encourage entrepreneurship and autonomy.** The organization is, for all practical purposes, divided into smaller companies and encouraged to think competitively and independently.
4. They evolve around the perspective of **productivity through people.** All employees are constantly reminded that their best performance is essential and they will share in the rewards of the organization.

5. **Supervisors are "hands-on" type individuals** who view one of their roles as shaping values. The staff is always very much in touch with the corporation's inner workings.
6. They concentrate on **doing what the company knows best.** They don't become involved with matters they do not understand.
7. Their **organizational structure is relatively simple.** Few high level administrators exist. The staff is lean, with only a small number of administrative layers.
8. An organizational **atmosphere promotes dedication to the basic values of the company.** At the same time, however, employees are permitted to be innovative in the way they follow these values.

APPLICATION TO THE POLICE

Careful reflection upon the preceding principles concludes the managerial framework proposed by *In Search of Excellence* can be successfully adapted to law enforcement. As Peters and Waterman point out, "moreover, we think readers may be pleasantly surprised to see how interesting the theory is. It is not, we would add, new or untested; most of the theory has stood the scientific test of time and defied refutation. It merely has been ignored, by and large, by managers and management writers." The same holds true with the police. Those agencies which ignore or refuse to implement managerial policies to improve performance and effectiveness become stagnant. Those that implement them surface as tomorrow's great leaders. Examples of how these principles may be applied to any police department can further a clearer understanding.

The first basic principle, action, is neither complex nor difficult to understand. In both the corporate world and law enforcement, some organizations consistently surface as role models. Others are satisfied with following the pacesetters. The difference is leadership. Progressive and innovative leaders constantly strive for improvement. They continue to move toward the future. They are neither afraid to make decisions or mistakes. When a mistake is made, it's simply viewed as a learning experience and the progressiveness continues.

In any given community, the leading law enforcement agencies are evident. They are the departments with administrators that are not afraid to make decisions. They are the ones who act as opposed to following others. An atmosphere of progressiveness and innovation is felt throughout every division and unit. These are the agencies that were the first in their community to try an employee counseling program, initiate the national accreditation process, develop a community service officer program or concentrate on human resource development.

The second basic principle is to "stay close to the customer." This crucial business principle is sometimes overlooked. It emphasizes the importance of determining the customer's needs, then satisfying them. Excellent companies appreciate the importance of this and do something about it. They also realize that satisfied customers produce a more than satisfactory profit margin.

Law enforcement's customer is of course the general public. Surveys and studies repeatedly conclude the majority of an agency's actual tasks are not law enforcement; they're community service. The manner and degree of service provided directly affects the degree of cooperation, financial support and community assistance each agency receives.

Unfortunately, whether they admit it or not, all experienced officers have witnessed other officers being unnecessarily rude or condescending with citizens. Administrators cannot tolerate such actions. In addition to reprimands or other forms of discipline, another solution is to foster the importance of helpfulness and professional courtesy toward citizens. If officers really appreciate the professional significance of being friendly or taking a little extra time to help in some small way, rudeness will significantly decrease. Yet, to overcome the initial resistance of many "street" officers, supervisors must be trusted and respected. Personal respect is impossible when supervisors aren't trusted.

The third principle involves autonomy and entrepreneurship. The best run organizations tend to be decentralized and filled with an entrepreneurial spirit. Even gigantic corporations such as IBM and 3M have organized themselves so they can "act small." The corporations are divided into so many small companies. These companies are encouraged to think independently and stimulate innovation.

As in the business world, police departments must find ways to stimulate innovation and creativity. New ideas and better ways of doing things should be generated in every division and unit. Administrators should understand the difference between creativity and innovation. An employee is creative if he thinks of new ideas or improvements. He is innovative if he is able to convert those new ideas into action. There are many more creative people than there are innovators. By knowing the difference, administrators can stimulate innovation.

Creative people often pass the responsibility for implementing their ideas to upper administration. Police chiefs and sheriffs need employees who take the time to make things happen. All too often someone has a good idea but is not willing to develop it into a practical benefit for the organization. "Idea men" constantly pepper everybody with proposals and memorandums which are just brief enough to get attention, intrigue and sustain interest—but too short to include any responsible suggestions for implementation. The scarce people are the ones who have the know-how, energy, daring and staying power to implement ideas. Since business is a "get-things-done" institution, creativity without follow through is a barren form of behavior. In a sense, it is irresponsible.[19] Law enforcement executives must strive to guarantee their agencies are filled with employees whose actions speak louder than words.

The fourth principle for excellence is that employees are an organization's most precious resource. The police are notorious for not taking care of their own. Some departments are managed by administrators who believe most employees are incompetent, incapable or inept. An underlying atmosphere of us (management) versus them (employees) is felt in every division. These are agencies where morale is low, distrust is prevalent and dedication is considered stupid—one in which managers enjoy supervision by fear and intimidation.

Of all the improvements a law enforcement administrator can make, the single most productive change would be to start treating employees as the highest priority of the organization. So many agencies still manage their personnel as if it were a military organization. Widespread belief exists that law enforcement agencies should be paramilitary. Military leaders have but one fundamental purpose: to lead soldiers into battle. Police, on the other hand, have much more varied responsibilities.

We now know, through analysis of our most productive organizations, that the classic theory X management style is little more than demoralizing and anti-productive. Administrators must rise above methods of the past and produce a tone of cooperation, dedication and employee betterment. Actions really do speak louder than words. Officers quickly become hostile and bitter when their administration claims to treat them well, yet does nothing to prove it. Improved employee treatment creates much greater dedication and loyalty. Increased dedication produces better job performance. The spirit of doing the best job possible will soon equate to professionalism.

The fifth principle for excellence is a "hands-on, value driven" management style. The business community appreciates the value of supervisors who stay close to the work at hand. A profile of Lee Iacocca's management style yields unique keys to his business success. The "hands-on" Iacocca was compelled to badger old-line Chrysler suppliers and unionists during the years that Chrysler was battling for federal loan guarantees with a crew of mutinous lenders. When K-cars arrived at the end of 1980, Chrysler could claim its warrantee costs had fallen slightly below those of Ford and were nearly comparable to those of GM.

The Quality-Control hammer yielded by Iacocca did not miss Chrysler's suppliers. Declaring that quality-control supervisors were a bargain when contrasted with the fallout of sloppy quality, they restored to purchasing a quality-control staff previously terminated by another company.

The transplantings and implantings of the Iacocca landscapers were taking root and producing results. The time had come to assure the first all-new products bearing the Iacocca signature — the Plymouth Reliant and the Dodge Aries K-cars — were in shape for the acid test of consumer acceptance. Otherwise, all the crash programs would have been in vain and Chrysler would be a dead duck.[20]

Research on truly excellent companies repeatedly concludes management should use a "hands-on" approach to supervision. Applying this to law enforcement simply means middle and upper level supervisors must get on the street and ride with officers, attend roll call and go to lunch with those they don't see very often. In other words, let the troops know you care about them and their problems.

One major weakness of many departments is easily remedied when supervisors substitute "hands-on" management in place of staying behind their desks. The weakness: a lack of meaningful values and ethics. Most police academies try hard, yet fail miserably, at engraving sound values. Most departments don't furnish any training on ethical considerations. Officers' ethics and values must originate from the top. All departments should display plaques and pictures of the law enforcement code of ethics and symbols of dedication throughout the station. Constant reminders, both in writing and verbally, will help to convince officers that supervisors are sincere when they speak of what it means to be a cop. Administrators must be sure that supervisors constantly stress ethics.

The sixth basic principle of excellence contends an organization should concentrate on matters it knows best. Research has determined those which go beyond areas of their expertise become less effective and efficient. Diversifying a wide variety of areas greatly lessens excellence. It's possible to "branch out," yet stay close to a basic expertise. Organizations that adhere to this greatly out perform those that are not.

Every officer has heard the phrase "patrol is the backbone of law enforcement." Many are laughing when they say this. Others are sarcastic. The reason—uniform patrol is typically viewed as an assignment officers want to transfer from. Being assigned to the "backbone" of the department includes bad hours, rain, cold, heat, frustration and endless sarcastic remarks. To make matters worse, officers no longer in patrol usually forget how bad the working conditions can be. They lose sight of the long hours of boredom and monotony. They forget the constant demeaning slurs and hostile stares officers face on the street.

Once again, actions speak louder than words. Administrators can do more than refer to patrol division as the "backbone." Priorities can be changed so other divisions and units do not receive higher priority or support. There are many ways of doing this. The solution means action as opposed to good intentions, rhetoric and procrastination. Stating the "street cop" will appreciate it is an understatement. The following are simple, yet effective ways of establishing a renewed emphasis on patrol:

1. **Paperwork** — Few things are more frustrating and irritating than repetitive paperwork. Conversely, streamlining report forms so useless information is deleted will have a very favorable effect on morale. In addition, officers will be "in-service" quicker. Many forms and/or sections of reports may be consolidated to make the officer's job faster and more efficient.

2. **Equipment** — Unlike other occupations, a uniform officer's office is the front seat of his patrol car. Anything the administration can do to enhance his equipment or working conditions is greatly appreciated. If need be, fund-raising or budgetary justification can focus on the danger to officers and citizenry if outdated or broken equipment is not replaced or repaired. Stressing the civil liability of poor equipment remaining in use should produce positive results.

3. **Field Training Officer Program** — Any law enforcement agency which does not have a field training officer program should immediately develop one. Most chiefs agree their FTO program is one of the most beneficial accomplishments they've ever achieved. A highly structured, well organized and committed FTO program is invaluable to the uniform patrol division.

4. **Career Tracking** — All police departments have a few patrolmen who enjoy their assignment so much they don't seek promotions for fear of reassignment. A career tracking program allows these officers to remain patrolmen, yet receive financial and non-

monetary recognition for their expertise. Many programs signify levels of patrolman: patrolman 1, patrolman 2, patrolman 3 and masterpatrolman. With each elevation in rank a pay raise and appropriate insignia is afforded. Every level requires passing a battery of competitive examinations and being on the department a specified number of years. Agencies that have career tracking would face a riot if it were disbanded.

5. **Community Service Officers** — A shortage of manpower is common in uniform divisions. The community service officer program can help. It's a good idea, that's long overdue. There's no reason why all agencies can't have community service officers. They respond to less complicated and non-dangerous calls, leaving full-time officers free for more serious calls. Simple thefts, traffic control, barking dogs, parking violations and various public service requests may be handled by community service officers. More appropriate allocation of sworn officers is a natural result. The benefits are obvious.

The seventh principle is keeping the administrative structure simple. Increased size usually causes ineffective complexity and needless bureaucracy. Many excellent companies have learned that "small is beautiful." Emerson Electric has 54,000 employees, yet less than 100 work at corporate headquarters. Schlumberger, a 6 billion dollar oil service company uses a corporate staff of only ninety. Ray Kroc, of McDonalds, states "I believe that less is more, in the case of corporate management." McDonalds has virtually no staff. All staff assignments are considered temporary and assigned to line officers. Sam Walton, the founder of Wal-Mart, believes in the empty headquarters rule: "The key is to get into stores and listen."[21]

What does all of this mean to law enforcement? It means administrators should reassess their organizational structure. It means a simple structure lends itself to a more effective organization. Furthermore, fewer mid-level supervisors make "hands-on" management much more workable. Currently, many supervisors spend their time doing nothing more than approving or disapproving the ideas of others. Imagine how efficient the handling of a typical memorandum would be if it only needs to pass through a two or three level chain of command as opposed to six or seven.

The eighth and last basic principle of excellence is to create a dedication to the organization's values, along with a tolerance for those who accept them. Having a sense of value has always had a great deal to do with ... and highly productive wor... ...lf-image and high esteem ... ...l direct the desire for peak ...

H... ...ms mundane employees t... ...s who are relentlessly positi... ...nes who look forward to wa... ...interest in employees and g... ...gency.

All ... ...hed, thoroughly understoo... ...rd operating procedures ... ...ctiveness of performance. ... ...les is crucial. The "rules" ... ...ve tone. Their emphasis i... ...perimentation and quality. ... ...cts of employment rather th... ...her hand, concentrate on ... ...e behavior. This is not to su... ...Actually, suspensions and reprimands should lessen because officers' behavior and self-discipline will improve.

Self-imposed discipline is merely one benefit of this management style. From the newest rookie to the old and crusty veteran, officers will be driven by renewed desire. The search for excellence will be over. Quality service, innovative problem solving and a genuine desire to do the best job possible will spread throughout the department. Individual shifts and divisions can thrive on internal competition. Internal communication and relationships will acquire a sincerity never before experienced. What's the hardest part of developing this tremendous style of management? The courage to take the first step.[22] It's so much easier to pretend apathy, and uncaring doesn't exist.

MOTIVATION FROM THE TOP

Quality job performance is an achievement which must start from the top and filter down throughout the organization. Study after study concludes employees are motivated more by how they are treated than by salary. Law enforcement's highest level administrators shouldn't wait any longer to abandon their bureaucratic management style and create an atmosphere that motivates employees to excel.

A sheriff or police chief who uses traditional management probably believes his employees must be ordered to work diligently, attempts to avoid work and isn't really dedicated to the goals of the organization. Though strict authoritarian supervision for police is appropriate under certain conditions, it's generally a very poor form of leadership.

One reason bureaucratic management styles are unproductive is that today's employees are different than those of the past. As previously noted, salary is not the main motivating force. America's current work force is inspired by feelings of accomplishment, the opportunity to "make a difference," self-esteem and deriving a sense of accomplishment. Having a chance to demonstrate what they can achieve is important to most people. Receiving some degree of recognition for a job well done perpetuates an even stronger desire to excel.

Law enforcement administration, like corporate management, will reap tremendous benefits from a participation management style. When it's given a chance, a total revitalization of attitude can filter throughout an organization. Problems like apathy, absenteeism, poor communications, poor interpersonal relationships and high turnover will begin to improve. Officers in every department across the nation are filled with unleashed potential. The key to unlocking it is the chief administrator.

The chief of police or sheriff is the key to success or the catalyst for failure because it is he who controls the tone of the organization. He's the one who set the atmosphere. Motivation starts at the top. Employees can be motivated by dedication to the agency, or be driven by self-serving interests. The staff will follow the policies and examples set by the chief administrator. Subordinates follow the examples of their immediate supervisor.

It's obvious which management style is compatible with professionalism. The police must have a staff with a sincere interest. Fear and intimidation have no place in a professional law enforcement agency. Domineering and inflexible supervisors will counteract any benefits derived by more enlightened supervisors. Inherently motivating staff members are those who:

1. Convey a sincere interest in others.
2. Satisfy the needs of subordinates.
3. Develop an organizational commitment.
4. Are honest and open in dealings with fellow employees.
5. Allow officers to play an active role in decision makings.
6. Provide challenges and responsibilities for officers.

7. Convey trust and understanding.
8. Assist in the personal development of employees.

THE HEWLETT-PACKARD EXAMPLE

The Hewlett-Packard Corporation manufactures sophisticated electronic products for distribution throughout the world. It was founded in 1939 by Dave Packard and Bill Hewlett, former classmates at Stanford University.

The Hewlett-Packard motivational leadership style is recognized throughout the world as an example of managerial excellence. From their initial conception of the corporation, Hewlett and Packard sought and developed a caring relationship between managers and employees. It has reaped monumental rewards. Bill Hewlett explains what has come to be known as the HP Way.

"It is the policies and actions that flow from the belief that men and women want to do a good job, a creative job, and they will do so if they are provided with the proper environment. That's part of it. Coupled closely with this is the HP tradition of treating each individual with consideration and respect and recognizing personal achievements. Dave Packard and I honestly believe this and have tried to operate the company guided by this philosophy since we started." [23]

The HP Way involves an assortment of interrelated strategies, all which foster harmony, togetherness and the desire to do your very best. Practically speaking, the theme of caring about employees can be implemented in many ways. There is absolutely no reason why the chief administrator of any police agency can't use the following managerial strategies. In doing so, he will be called a leader with foresight and wisdom. Rightfully so, for he will be the one who's taken the initiative, progressiveness and determination to forge the path for others to follow.

The HP Way

Incentives and Rewards — an informal, practical approach to provide employees with a variety of incentives and rewards is considered crucial to the Hewlett-Packard Way. Whether it is an unexpected check for a hundred dollars or a day off with pay, outstanding work is rewarded. Having a supervisor tell an employee he has been doing a great job is important. When he also says please accept a check as a token of gratitude, it is an event he'll never forget. Irregardless of the amount of money, being recognized for outstanding performance is invaluable to an individual's self-esteem and ego.

Some departments have an internal newsletter. Those that do not should develop one. In addition to encouraging comradeship and harmony, it is a fantastic method of delivering recognition for top performance. Special attention can be given to those who remain dedicated, reliable and hardworking. While not as obvious as someone who accomplished a single outstanding task or reacted heroically in a dangerous situation, loyal, hardworking officers shouldn't go unnoticed.

Management by Wandering Around — There's a management technique at HP they term management by wandering around. It's based on the fact that the most important facets of any operation occur at the point where the work takes place, as opposed to a supervisor's office. Thus, managers get out from behind their desks and talk with others about how day-to-day operations are going. The atmosphere is casual and relaxed. The tone is sincere and grateful. The purpose is to listen and help. The results are real and evident.

Everyone at Hewlett-Packard refers to others by their first name. The atmosphere is very informal. Managers don't have luxurious offices. No one needs to make an appointment with a supervisor; his door is always open. No suggestion box exists. Workers know that no matter what the problem or idea, they will always feel comfortable speaking with their supervisor. They also appreciate the fact they're encouraged to do so.

Physical Environment — Any visitor walking through Hewlett-Packard immediately notices it's not a typical company. The warmth and friendly atmosphere is evident. The sterile office environment is absent. No restrictions limit personal photographs or decor in a desk area as long as they don't interfere with work. The HP Way includes allowing workers to create a comfortable and warm, home-like atmosphere. It is simply another way of showing employees they care. It costs nothing, yet means so much.

Worker Security — Having job security is an invaluable asset. It means you'll never be terminated unjustly and every effort will be made to prevent any employee from being laid off.

An example of how strongly Hewlett-Packard believes in providing job security occurred in 1970. The company would experience financial losses unless they reduced labor expenses by a minimum of 10 percent. While most companies facing similar situations would terminate employees, Hewlett-Packard found another way. The solution was to have everyone, including Hewlett and Packard, take a day off without pay every two weeks. The schedule returned to normal when business increased in a few months. The incident proved to employees that no matter how tough business may get, the company will always be behind them. It was still another example of the trust and loyalty among all levels of the organization.

Caring — Eugene Benge and John Hickey, in their book, *Morale and Motivation,* describe Hewlett-Packard's management style as "selfishly altruistic." In other words, they are convinced the most effective way of deriving high profit is to manage people with an untiring devotion to their welfare. Furthermore, the HP Way works. It has been hailed by numerous contemporary management texts such as *In Search of Excellence* as a model to follow.

An example of true caring is found in the center of a production area. It is there that an advisor may be located. The advisor serves to help employees with any type problem bothering them. From family situations to financial matters, the counselor remains a good listener. He follows through by doing whatever possible to find a solution. Caring for each other is stressed throughout; it is simply another part of the HP Way.

Training — Hewlett-Packard believes in continuous training. Besides formal programs, they've devised a method of immediate, one-on-one, intensive training. When someone is having a problem of some type, a lead employee is immediately assigned to assist him. Because lead worker's assume additional responsibilities, they are frequently rewarded with supervisory positions.[24] This method of training offers immediate, personal instruction while fostering employee relationships.

CAREER DEVELOPMENT

One of the similarities of all excellent companies is that they appreciate the importance of developing the human resources of their employees. Times have changed, effective managers now realize people need more than fear to keep them working efficiently over long periods of time. Human resource development is widely recognized in business circles.

One of the mainstays of human resource development is career development. When an employee, assisted by his employer, determines his short and long range career goals, the process is termed career planning. The outcome of this type of planning is known as career development. Any employee performs better if he believes his career is aimed in the proper direction. The corporate community understands that success is greatly dependent on how well the organization develops and uses the skills, knowledge and abilities of its employees.

Effective career development can only result from the collaborative efforts of an employee and his organization. It's an ongoing process that is continually refined with the assistance of supervisors and/or the human resource development unit. Career counseling helps employees merge their personal goals with organizational needs.

All effective career development programs include certain components. First, the agency must assess its need for career development. Second, it obtains the needed information. Lastly, it develops a plan of action.

Career development needs assessment must be well organized and thorough. Failing to conduct a competent assessment will result in little more than a waste of time and misleading information on which future decisions are based. Competent needs analysis can prevent this. It assists in developing programs that are relevant, effective, well received and long lasting. No specific career development program is suitable for all organizations; every organization has different cultures and needs.

The needs assessment requires three phases: a procedure for determining the ideal career development system, a method to determine the effectiveness of your present system, and a manner of deciding upon programs to bridge the gap between the two.

Obtaining input from various internal sources provides the most realistic assessment obtainable. Both written questionnaires and interviews with supervisors and subordinates are necessary. Those new to career development may feel stymied while determining proper topics for their needs assessment. The following model will help to assure that the assessment is effective. It can be used to promote group discussions or individual interviews. Advisory committees may find it useful in making recommendations for future career development programs. Lastly, the model should be beneficial in developing and organizing a career development records system.[25]

TOPICS FOR CAREER DEVELOPMENT
NEEDS ASSESSMENT

I. Information for Individuals

    A. About themselves:

        • Interests, skills and values.

        • An awareness that the organization expects them to be responsible and active.

- Strengths and weaknesses of their present job performance.
- The roles or responsibilities the organization allows and wants them to take.
- Their current career stage, career goals and career plans.

B. About their organization:
  - Job openings, requirements and salaries.
  - Career paths in the organization.
  - How the informal system works.
  - Role and responsibility of the organization in their career management.
  - Organization's goals, values, plans and their effect.
  - Developmental resources the company offers.
  - How the organization feels about their potential and its plans for them.

II. Information for the Organization
  A. About itself:
    - Present and future jobs.
    - Job requirements.
    - Company's past career development activities.
    - Future economic, political and social trends that can affect it.
    - Historical information such as job trends, past growth trends and company's beginning.
    - Future goals.
    - Values.
    - Who is leaving and why.
    - Promotional and pay policies.
    - Methods offered to develop and help employees.
    - Which programs and practices are effective.
    - Role in employee career development.

  B. About employees:
    - Who it employs, their ages and other personal data.
    - How well they are performing, their strengths, weaknesses and potential.
    - Employee training, education, interests, goals, plans, skills and values.
    - Historical information on each person's career, inside and outside the company.
    - Whether the employee understands the "system"; the formal and informal policies and procedures.

III. Ways of Getting, Maintaining and Using Information
  A. Personnel data records for each individual containing:
    - Information on age, education, length of service and past jobs outside the company.
    - Company job history.
    - Training while at the company.

- Performance appraisal review (skills and weaknesses).
- Development plans.
- Interests and long-range career plans of employees, and
- Assessments of potential.

B. A career-pathing program that entails:
- Job analysis.
- Written job descriptions.
- Job evaluation showing relevant worth and salary relevance, and
- Historical movements of employees from past
- Promotion records and transfer interviews and records.

C. A manpower planning system for assessing human resources quantitatively and qualitatively that includes:
- Forecasting that examines quantitative assessment.
  - Current openings identified and compared with current manpower resources, and
  - Future openings and required manpower identified in connection with organizational and strategic planning.
- Succession planning based on qualitative assessment.
  - Current human resources assessed on skills, development needs and potential using one or more of the following:
- Assessment centers.
- Self-assessment.
- Performance appraisals by supervisors.
- Individual assessment by supervisor and/or others, and
- Committee (team) or peer assessment.
  - Candidates for future positions identified and offered developmental activities as preparation.

D. A supervisor-employee relationship that includes:
- Performance appraisal through feedback to employees and feedback to the organization about the individual:
- Career discussion that involves:
  - Information to the employee about the organization;
  - Information to the organization about the employee in the form of a career plan, interests, and goals;
  - Support, encouragement, and realistic feedback on career plans to the individual; and
  - Coaching by the supervisor, serving as a role model or a mentor.

E. Career counseling by people in the personnel section that may give information to the employee about the organization and self-assessment through tests that clarify skills, interests, and values.

F. Counseling by outside professionals.

G. Career workbooks completed by employees independently and allow employees to write out career plans.

H. Methods of information exchange that includes media, pamphlets, tapes, booklets, and newsletters.

I. Upper management communication of information, philosophy and support, such as luncheon speeches and meetings.

J. Career workshops and seminars that
- Train supervisors and employees on roles and responsibilities and needed skills.
- Offer career assessment and planning techniques.
- Provide information on the company, and
- Help clarify values.

K. An internal system for promotion and movement includes job posting or other self-nominating methods and promotions, lateral transfers, and downward moves.

L. Developmental opportunities that involves:
- Internal company sponsored classes.
- OJT or apprenticeship.
- Job rotation.
- Sabbaticals and seminars.
- Outside classes.
- Formal education.
- Programmed instruction.
- Self-directed study.
- Special assignments.
- Mentors.
- Immediate supervisors.
- Other than immediate supervisors.
- Financial support (tuition refund), and
- Membership and involvement in professional associations.

M. A monitoring system that entails evaluation of the career development methods used and opinions and attitudes of the employees.

N. A reward system which includes wage and salary based on job worth and achievement; and recognition, benefits, and rewards appropriate to the values of organization and employees.

IV. A Supportive Climate and an Open Communication Style That Uses:

A. Ongoing participation of employees and management in the design and revision of the career development system.

B. Honesty by employees and management about the career development system.

C. Openness and mutual concern that generates high level of trust.

D. A free flow of information about the career development system and other organizational systems, and

E. A mutual willingness by employees, management, and the organization to adjust needs and expectations based on practicality and reality.[26]

THE CAREER TRACK PROGRAM

Law enforcement agencies have never been good at "taking care" of their officers. Most officers across America agree that police work is stressful. What may be surprising to people outside law enforcement is that most officers feel the majority of their stress is created within their organization, rather than on the street. Most police departments operate within a structure that requires officers to assume command positions to achieve career growth. The fallacy of this traditional system is that many capable officers become unnecessarily frustrated due to the limited number of staff openings.

Failing to have an adequate career development process frequently produces several negative conditions. The following frustrations are very detrimental to any organization:

1. Highly qualified and proficient employees are frequently forced to leave appropriate assignments to accept promotions.
2. Employee stagnation and a decrease in productivity is considered normal.
3. Many of any agency's top performers will resign due to the lack of advancement potential.
4. Devastating internal politics increase as competition for the relatively few promotions creates hard feelings and jealousy among employees.

A career track program eliminates the causes of career frustration by rewarding high achieving employees. It recognizes high performance in areas such as increased personal skills, job knowledge and abilities of operational personnel. Ever increasing levels of professionalism are achieved as officers mature both personally and professionally. Continued maturity is encouraged through challenging training and structured experiences.

The Altamonte Springs, Florida Police Department, under the guidance of Chief of Police, William A. Liquori, implemented a career track program in 1982. In doing so, they demonstrated the progressiveness necessary for law enforcement to rise above mediocrity and achieve true professionalism. Like most innovative programs, career tracking requires a commitment to professionalism and the courage to take a chance. For a career track program to be successful, the agency must provide appropriate training, be actively supported by all levels of management and furnish needed monetary resources.

The Altamonte model is based upon a straight line career progression from "Probationary Patrolman" to "Master Patrolman." The progression evolves around formalized tests and demonstrated achievement of the prerequisites. It does not cross the individual into command responsibilities. Although the rewards of command may be greater, the availability of these positions is much more limited.

THE CAREER TRACK COMPONENTS

A. **The Patrolman Second Class** — This position is the first step of the Operational Career Track. Sworn officers may elect to compete for this position should they meet the following criteria:

(1) A minimum of three years continuous sworn service with the department, irrespective of unit assignment.

(2) In the preceding 12 months, the employee must have achieved an overall evaluation of "above average" or better. No individual category within the evaluation can be rated as "below average" or "unsatisfactory." In the case of an officer who has been transferred within the above time frame, his evaluation qualification will be based on the 12-month time frame prior to his transfer.

(3) In the preceding 12 months, the employee must not have received any "formal" discipline. By definition, formal discipline is construed as punitive in nature, not educational, and is normally reserved for repeated minor violations or for more serious transgressions.

Once the prerequisites have been achieved, the employee may apply to compete in the testing process. The Patrolman Second Class test is composed of the following elements:

(1) A written test concerning department and city policies, procedures, rules and regulations.

(2) A written test concerning commonly used statutes, ordinances and elements of crimes.

(3) An in-basket exercise consisting of various reports. In this exercise the candidate must identify and correct errors.

At the conclusion of the testing process, candidates achieving a final score of 70 percent are listed as eligible for promotion. The chief of police may select any officer on the list in awarding promotions.

B. **The Patrolman First Class** — This position is the second step within the Operational Career Track. Sworn officers may elect to compete for this position should they meet the following criteria:

(1) A minimum of three years continuous sworn service with the department, as a patrolman second class, irrespective of unit assignment.

(2) In the preceding 12 months, the employee must have achieved an overall evaluation of "above average" or better. No individual category within the evaluation can be rated as "below average" or "unsatisfactory." In the case of an officer who has been transferred within the above time frame, his evaluation qualification will be based on the 12-month time frame prior to the transfer.

(3) For the preceding 12 months, the employee must not have received any "formal" discipline.

Once the prerequisites have been achieved, the employee may apply to compete in the testing process. The patrolman first class test is composed of the following elements:

(1) A written test concerning department and city policies, procedures, rules and regulations.

(2) A written test concerning commonly used statutes, ordinances and elements of crimes.

(3) An in-basket exercise consisting of various reports. In this exercise, the candidate must identify and correct errors.

(4) A role-playing exercise that requires the candidate to demonstrate interpersonal skills appropriate to the position.

At the conclusion of the testing process, candidates achieving a final score of 75 percent are listed as eligible for promotion. The chief of police may select any officer on the list when awarding promotions.

C. **The Master Patrolman** — This position is the third step within the Operational Career Track. Sworn officers may elect to compete for this position, should they meet the following criteria:

(1) A minimum of three years continuous sworn service with the department, as a patrolman first class, irrespective of unit assignment.

(2) In the preceding 18 months, the employee must have achieved an overall evaluation of "above average" or better. No individual category within the evaluation can be rated as "below average" or "unsatisfactory." In the case of an officer who has been transferred during the above time frame, the evaluation qualification will be based on an 18-month time frame prior to their transfer.

(3) For the preceding 18 months, the employee must not have been awarded "formal" discipline.

Once the prerequisites have been achieved, the employee may apply to compete in the testing process. The master patrolman test is composed of the following elements:

(1) A written test concerning department and city policies, procedures, rules, regulations, local government structure and concepts.

(2) A written test on selected statutes, elements of crime and interpretation of statutes and related court decisions.

(3) An in-basket exercise consisting of various reports in which the candidate must identify and correct errors.

(4) A role-playing exercise that requires the candidate to demonstrate interpersonal skills appropriate to the position.

(5) Preparation of a police operational plan requiring the candidate to demonstrate his skills in planning, deployment and utilization of resources.

At the conclusion of the testing process, candidates achieving a final score of 80 percent are listed as eligible for promotion. The chief of police may select any officer on the list in awarding the promotion.

As with any promotional testing process, it is crucial that the agency ensure reliability and validity.

The command staff may develop the tests used in the model, based upon the tasks performed by members of the department.

A. **Written Tests** — Each position in the career track incorporates a written test within the testing module. This test differs in complexity and difficulty for each position, but the format is the same — objective. The questions are either true/false, multiple choice, or "fill in the blank" type. They are drawn directly from source materials supplied the candidate a minimum of 60 days prior to the test date.

At the conclusion of the test, each question is analyzed. Should a significant number of candidates miss a particular question, it is reviewed by the staff to determine if a problem exists with the question. Questions are voided and credited each candidate as appropriate. Candidates are also allowed to challenge any question they feel is unfair.

B. **The In-Basket Exercise** — Each position within the career track incorporates an in-basket exercise. As this process is designed for operational units, the command staff designs the exercise. It consists of numerous police reports and forms. These forms contain numerous errors. The object of the exercise to identify and correct the mistakes.

This exercise specifically tests candidate skills in:

1. Report writing and editing.

2. Knowledge of statutes.
3. Knowledge of city and department procedures.

At the conclusion of the test, each response is analyzed. Should a significant number of candidates miss a particular point, it is reviewed by the staff to reassess its creditability. Points may be voided or credited each candidate as appropriate. Candidates are also allowed to challenge any point they feel is unfair.

C. **The Role-Playing Exercise** — The patrolman first class and master patrolman testing modules include a role-playing exercise.

A scenario is prepared which requires each candidate to demonstrate interpersonal skills. A role-player is recruited, usually from an outside agency, to serve as the catalyst for the process. A minimum of three assessors are selected and trained to evaluate the candidates in the following areas:

1. Demeanor and appearance.
2. Oral communication skills.
3. Stress tolerance.
4. Ability/persuasiveness.
5. Sensitivity.
6. Listening skills.
7. Flexibility.
8. Control.
9. Problem analysis and alternatives.
10. Overall judgement.

Each of the ten dimensions evaluated are scored on a scale of one to ten. Scoring is done independently by each assessor. They are then combined and a mean average is determined.

After the mean average of all candidates is obtained, the difference between it and the minimum passing score is determined. If the mean score of the candidates is below the minimum passing score, the difference is credited with each score. In effect, this process arbitrarily moves the mean score of the candidates to equal the minimum passing score for the exercise.

D. **The Operational Plan** — For the position of master patrolman, the concerned test requires the officer to develop an operational plan. This component determines the ability of the candidate to plan, organize, staff and control a hypothetical event.

In preparing the exercise, the command staff composes a scenario, then develops a model plan. When completed, every specific point of action is evaluated as a necessary (mandatory) or optional police response. The process creates a scoring system of mandatory actions with which candidate's plans can be compared and graded.

In scoring the plans, it's possible for alternatives to be presented that weren't in the original plan. These are reviewed and credit is given if the answer is appropriate.

Staffing Requirements

Depending upon the size and management philosophy of the agency, the number of positions authorized within the career track may vary. The method of determining the number of positions is a matter of discretion.

In the Altamonte model, management wanted the ability to reward employees who provide higher than average performance. Thus, the positions were determined through the following formula. It should be noted that the formula provides only the number of positions available to be filled, not the actual number of employees promoted.

A. **Patrolman Second Class** — The number of authorized PSC positions is equal to one half of the number of patrolman positions authorized for the department.

For example: 100 authorized patrolmen divided by two equals 50 authorized PSC positions.

B. **Patrolman First Class** — The number of authorized PFC positions is equal to one half the number of patrolman second class positions.

For example: 50 authorized PSC positions divided by two equals 25 authorized patrolman first class positions.

C. **Master Patrolman** — The number of authorized master patrolman positions is equal to one fourth the number of patrolman first class positions.

For example: 25 authorized PFC positions divided by four equals 6.25 or 6 authorized master patrolman positions.

Each position within the career track relates to an assigned pay grade within the city pay plan. Every promotion within the career track creates a five percent pay adjustment. Promotions of officers within the career track into command positions generates an increase in pay as follows:

- From patrolman to watch commander   20 percent
- From patrolman second class to watch commander   15 percent

- From patrolman first class to watch commander   10 percent
- From master patrolman to watch commander   5 percent

Using this mathematical process in determining position availability allows the career track to develop with growth of the department. Failing to allow for adjustment required by growth may limit the ability of the system to meet its objectives. Additionally, the system can be easily replicated by any size department.

Summary

The effects of employee career frustration are detrimental to any organization and can be partially attributed to inattentive personnel management.

To attract and maintain high achieving employees, it's necessary to provide for employee growth through recognition and advancement opportunity.

The Altamonte Springs Career Track was designed to furnish advancement opportunities for sworn officers without requiring assumption of command. It's based on a straight line career progression from "probationary patrolman" to "master patrolman." The progression is possible following satisfactory performance in a formal testing process which involves increased personal skills, job knowledge and abilities. A series of rigid prerequisites must be met by an employee prior to competing for the promotion.

The program can be replicated easily in any size law enforcement agency, if the agency is willing to make the necessary commitment. To succeed, the plan requires departments to furnish work experiences that provide the basis for increasing employee skills, job knowledge and abilities. Concurrently, training must be challenging and reinforce officer's professional growth.

The career track becomes immensely valuable to employees in terms of recognition and growth. It's also important to the department regarding effective personnel management and improved service delivery by better trained, more professional employees.

Although the career track generally relates to operational personnel, some management traits are tested. Acquiring and disseminating management skills is, of course, beneficial to every department. Officers involved in career tracking may be used to fill in command vacancies created by vacation, illnesses, training, etc. Although the time spent in these fill-in positions is minimal, it's also beneficial for the employee.

Such benefits increase proportionally in smaller departments due to a smaller pool of available command officers.

HUMAN RESOURCE DEVELOPMENT

Following the decrease in American productivity during the 1970's, business authors began to write highly developed and remarkably enlightened books regarding the American managerial awakening. Several references have been made to Peters and Waterman's *In Search of Excellence* (1982). Other notable works include *The Art of Japanese Management,* by Richard T. Pascale and Anthony G. Athos (1981), *The One Minute Manager,* by Kenneth Blanchard and Spencer Johnson (1981), *Theory Z,* by William Ouchi (1981) and *Leaders — The Strategies for Taking Charge,* by Warren Bennis and Burt Namus (1985). Though having a wider business scope, *Megatrends,* by John Naisbitt (1982), offered future perspectives and insights of managerial importance.

The central underlying theme most of these and other contemporary management texts have in common is that team work, sincerity, cooperation, respect and pride in one's work are the keys to a successful and effective organization. Nurturing and developing the personal skills and abilities of all employees, combined with renewed commitment and dedication will excel productivity to new found dimensions. Human resource development has become an unsung hero to many organizations.

Don't be fooled by those who claim because the research and conclusions were gathered from the corporate world, they can't apply or be successful in law enforcement. The police historically lagged behind the efficiency of America's most productive companies because they haven't put forth the initiative or courage to try new ideas. Some agencies will continue to ignore more productive supervisory techniques and keep burying their heads in the sand. The public and private sectors deal with many common concerns and resources. The same solutions can work for both.

The adage, "people make the world go around," seems oddly adaptable to the key for management success: people. How an agency's personnel are treated and developed is the key to success. Reorganizing an organizational structure and committing oneself to a new manner of thinking is crucial. Today's professional law enforcement administrators must acquire an appreciation for human resource development.

Without a foundation of fundamental HRD elements and subsequent benefits, an agency's true potential will never be reached.

HRD — WHAT IS IT? WHY HAVE IT?

Virtually all organizations have three types of resources: financial, physical and human. How administrators manage these resources is critical to the success of the organization. Properly managing human resources is rewarding, challenging and difficult.

Beyond the definition that human resource development implies, attempts to define the term have met with an assortment of responses. HRD is a broadly conceived field. It may involve anything from a single training course to very complex training systems that have been developed to meet specific goals and objectives. In general, however, HRD is any activity that produces the learning of skills or behavior on the part of employees or organizations. It includes a broad range of activities which result in learning and development.

Human resource development has been quietly growing in America since the 1940's. The business community now considers it an important component of corporate success. It's now developed beyond isolated attempts to teach specific skills, to include complex learning systems for improving critical organizational weaknesses. In doing so, it meets the highly competitive challenges of a global market place. HRD plays a major role in reaching the goals of a corporation competing in a competitive world market.

Just as an HRD unit serves the goals of a corporation, it may serve those of a law enforcement agency. The ability to train and develop police officers effectively is critical. Unlike a training division, an HRD unit encompasses a much wider scope of endeavors. Employees are not only trained. Instead, all of their skills, abilities and knowledge are nurtured and enhanced. Both to the employee's and the organization's benefit.

Naisbitt and Aburdine emphasize how much contemporary corporations appreciate the potential for human resource development in their book, *Reinventing the Corporation.* "In the new information society, human capital has replaced dollar capital as the strategic resource. People and profits are inexorably linked." Unlike the police culture, the business community recognizes and appreciates the value of human resources. This is evident in the thinking of business leaders, theorists, politicians, economists, business school curriculum, written media and the nation's best run companies.[27]

Transferring the well established HRD principles of business to law enforcement will be an enormous benefit. It will take us another step closer to professionalism. The following facts may be useful to administrators seeking budgetary approval for implementing an HRD unit in his agency.

Facts About Human Resource Development

- Nine of ten of America's largest companies (89 percent) designate a chief human resource executive at the corporate level.
- In a 1985 study, six out of ten employers had started new internal training programs in the previous two years.
- Employee participation in training programs has increased during the past five years. The number of training professionals has increased as well. For example, participation of first line supervisors increased 40 percent.
- Several million American workers are covered by union bargaining agreements that contain requirements for education and training.
- Of the 40 million new jobs created during the past fifteen years, only 5 to 6 million were in high-technology areas. The real challenge to training and development is the need to prepare America's workers for an information age and a service economy. By the year 2000, 75 percent of all employees will require retraining.
- Training and development is comparable to higher education in complexity and nearly equal in volume.
- Training and development — $210 billion per year.
- Formal education — $238 billion per year.
- Health care — $355 billion per year.
- Employee training by employers is the largest delivery system for adult education.
- As of 1985, 18 corporations were offering college-level degree programs. By 1988, at least 13 more corporations will be operating their own colleges.
- It is training, not formal education, that provides most job skills.
- Formal education accounts for only a 15 percent variation in lifetime earnings, compared to 85 percent generated by work-place learning.
- Training furnishes most skills acquired after the age of 25 and all skills for two out of three jobs.[28]

ORGANIZING AN HRD UNIT

It wouldn't be presumptuous to claim most police administrators will appreciate the value of human resource development after understanding the facts. Many will want to become immediately involved so their agency will yield the benefits as soon as possible. Having training division employees become active members in the American Society For

Training and Development, Alexandria, VA., is a very easy, effective and practical manner of involvement. ASTD offers many avenues through which the police may enlighten themselves to HRD methodology. Almost every location in the nation is represented by local chapters.

Following a sincere commitment, administrators must make sure their agency adopts an HRD policy. The policy should include an HRD mission and purpose statement, the unit's goals and objectives, a statement of organizational philosophy, establish managerial authority and create criteria for logistic matters. Though some organizations have been successful without it, policy statements encourage cooperation and team work among management. HRD managers will find that justifying various projects and proposals will be easier if a statement of policy is well established. The following sample policy is intended as a guide for developing your own HRD policy.

A Sample HRD Policy Statement

It shall be the policy of the Anywhere Law Enforcement Agency to recognize the importance of its employees, acknowledge their valued contributions to its mission, and place consistent emphasis on the management of human resource development. In the furtherance of this policy, the Anywhere Law Enforcement Agency shall:

1. Make continual effort to ensure that no employees are overlooked or exempted from HRD activities.
2. Emphasize and acknowledge the need for uninterrupted learning opportunities which are consistent with the organization's long range mission, goals and human resource requirements.
3. Acknowledge its responsibilities to furnish appropriate HRD learning opportunities (training, education and development) to employees and members of the management team. Furthermore, to assist employees in gaining or updating their technical skills and knowledge, and developing necessary managerial skills to the highest possible level in the search for excellence of performance.
4. Develop and administer HRD activities in a manner that provides both managerial and technical skills for all employees, in close cooperation with the management team.
5. Actively encourage participation in support of the full range of HRD activities by all employees. It must be emphasized that supervisors and managers at all levels are ultimately responsible for implementing learning activities that ensure employees perform at the highest levels of competence.
6. Establish priorities for participation in the organization's HRD activities so that special consideration is given to:

a. Employees who need additional technical or managerial skills to improve their effectiveness in carrying out presently assigned or future responsibilities.

b. Newly hired employees or members of the management team who require new job skills, knowledge or attitudes in the performance of their positions.

c. Employees who have established career goals and commitment to the organization are encouraged to remain employed in the organization for a time that is sufficient to warrant a return on the investment in their development.

d. Employees who are identified as possessing the greatest long range potential for advancement to high level assignments in the organization.[29]

Certainly, establishing an HRD policy is important. However, even the best intended policies will do little good if an organization is riddled with poor people oriented management. Law enforcement has, and continues to have, its share of poor leadership. The classic theory X management style often destroys the dedication and desire of many good officers. It's necessary to assess and honestly evaluate the way people are treated within your organization before HRD can improve it.

Assessing the past and current "organizational climate" can be a difficult task. It requires deep and open honesty to objectively examine your organization and yourself. It usually mandates candid conversations with employees at all levels. You may find the truth hurts. You may realize insecure or embittered supervisors were allowed to unfairly impose their animosities upon shifts or divisions of your organization. You may be forced to admit that it was you who should have taken steps to right supervisory injustices. Lastly, only you are the one who can change it.

Most adults have had experiences with or known of supervisors who believe employees are nothing more than disposable machines. Such supervisors thrive in organizations where employees are threatened with, "If you don't like it, there's the door." The administrators of these agencies must have the courage to admit their failings and drive ahead to invoke an enhanced work environment. Though the road may be long, remarkable improvement from human resource development will occur. Changes so astounding that those having felt trapped in an atmosphere of bitterness and distrust will literally have to see it to believe it. Don't feel a change of this magnitude can occur "overnight." It's a long process that **must** start at the top and work down. Supervisors must set an example for all to follow. Actions speak louder than words.

Irregardless of the status of an agency's internal atmosphere, HRD is crucial to it's effectiveness even if the administration is presently unfamiliar with HRD. As alluded to in *In Search of Excellence,* supervisors must be a good coach. This requires empathy and an ability to be sensitive to employees' needs. It is one of the least understood and appreciated managerial roles. A good coach is able to sense what employees need, then call upon his initiative and caring to satisfy it.

The managerial tasks of a good coach are synonymous with the principles of sound human resource development. Anything done to create a productive and satisfying work environment will increase the efficiency of the agency. The following are examples an administrator may use while explaining to his staff what techniques will yield the greatest potential from employees.

1. Developing human potential requires management that's responsive and supportive to the needs of employees.
2. Human resource development means helping, caring and providing positive feedback to subordinates.
3. Take a sincere interest in the personal lives of subordinates. Show sincere interest in supporting hobbies or other personal interests which makes an employee happy.
4. Instead of ordering or telling employees something in an intimidating tone, suggest ways he or she could have handled the situation better. Offer methods which may improve future performance. Devise role playing situations which allow subordinates to discover for themselves how alternative methods would be more appropriate.

Organizing An HRD Unit

Organizing an HRD unit is a unique undertaking. First, since most agencies don't currently have one, the potential for misconceptions spreading throughout the agency is high. Second, though it's crucial that many HRD activities occur within line areas, it is not a line division, itself. Even so, an HRD unit is not staffed in the usual sense because it involves both research and planning, along with the daily operations of the agency. Most enlightened administrators agree, an HRD unit is most appropriately structured as a staff position.

The role of an HRD unit essentially concerns servicing the learning needs of employees. More specifically, the components of training, career development, personal development and education. Some units, however, do little more than offer internal training or provide external specialized courses.

Law enforcement executives should ensure HRD managers organize the unit so it embraces the agency's overall goals and objectives. A variety of internal programs may be developed which go beyond police training needs. Programs that express sincerity and caring toward employees must be offered. As an example, the author knows of one police department's HRD unit that has a video tape library of 300 training tapes. The unusual aspect, however, is that a portion of the library has nothing to do with police training. These tapes focus on the personal development of officers. They involve everything from car repair, care of your newborn child, to basic cooking skills and spanish.

Some police administrators may view a human resource development unit as nothing more than a training division with a few additional responsibilities. This can be a devastating mistake because such a narrow view doesn't come close to adequately encompassing the unit's purpose. Some training supervisors may not have a temperament compatible with HRD principles. The manager must possess a sincerity that will be evident to all throughout the agency.

The HRD supervisor is responsible for conducting an agency's needs assessment. From a training perspective, besides those topics normally covered, special emphasis must be directed toward staff development to change any negative or anti-productive attitudes. From the perspective of career and personal development, supervisory programs that promote an atmosphere of cooperation and teamwork, while developing the qualities of all employees are desired.

Developing human potential or improving the atmosphere of a department is unlikely if thorough planning isn't done during initial stages of the process. Considerable planning is necessary: training schedules, budgetary consideration, utilization of facilities and equipment, staff allocation, management style changes, documentation procedures and individual career/personal development plans.

Effective planning allows HRD activities to be proactive as opposed to be reactive. Overall plans should be consistent with the goals and objectives of the agency. This is done by implemented HRD programs which help to resolve problems of productivity through well developed and implemented learning programs. An effective HRD unit will also plan to assist line and staff managers in the development of their subordinates' human resources by furnishing direct and thorough support services.[30]

HRD in the Fortune 500

HRD professionals, Lenny Ralphs and Eric Stephan, conducted research concerning human resource development practices within Fortune 500 companies. Particular focus was given in the areas of evaluation, needs analysis and training methods. The results offer the following insights:

1. The respondents overwhelmingly agree that technical training will grow substantially during the next several years.
2. Respondents feel improving communications is the most important management training topic.
3. They believe the most important HRD issue during the next five years will be "to have an excellent knowledge of the business and strategic plans of the company."
4. Respondents consider job-posting the most used career development tactic.
5. They believe that technological changes will have a greater impact on human resource development in the future than economic, social or political changes.

Some of the specific questions and subsequent answers by the Fortune 500 HRD professionals included the following:

1. When you think of Human Resource Development, which of the following would you consider to be subparts of the following?

Training and development	98 percent
Career development	94 percent
Human resource planning	89 percent
Organization development	86 percent
Staffing/recruiting	72 percent
Organization/job design	70 percent
Employee assistance	57 percent
Personnel research and Information systems	55 percent
Compensation/benefits	46 percent
Union/labor relations	40 percent

2. In your opinion, whose responsibility is the development of human resources?

a. Line management	63 percent
b. HRD professionals	37 percent

3. Do you now have a formal executive development program/system in place?

a. Yes	51 percent
b. No	37 percent

4. Do you have training for middle managers?
   a. Yes   91 percent
   b. No   6 percent

5. What percentage of the total training in your company is technical in comparison to all other training (such as management and sales training)?
   a. Technical training   44 percent
   b. All other training   56 percent

6. Do you expect technical training needs to grow, decline, or remain the same in your company in the next one to three years?
   a. Grow   74 percent
   b. Decline   2 percent
   c. Remain the same   22 percent

7. Do you have secretarial/clerical training in your company?
   a. Yes   56 percent
   b. No   34 percent

8. Do you have career development systems in your organization?
   a. Yes   62 percent
   b. No   28 percent

9. Do you use external consultants for your human resource development programs?
   a. Yes   85 percent
   b. No   9 percent

10. What percentage of your total human resource development is delivered by external consultants or training sources?

                          27 percent

11. What percentage of the skills learned in a course are lost without follow-up coaching?

                          69 percent

12. What percentage of the total HRD monetary resources are dedicated to the following areas in your company?
   a. Executive development   10 percent
   b. Middle management development   20 percent
   c. First line supervisory development   20 percent
   d. Sales training   13 percent
   e. Technical training   19 percent
   f. Secretarial/clerical   5 percent

13. Which of the following technological advances are being used for training in your company?
   a. Satellite TV networks   9 percent
   b. Teleconferencing   19 percent
   c. Interactive video   36 percent
   d. Computer assisted instruction   44 percent

e. Electronic workbooks   3 percent
f. Artificial intelligence   8 percent[31]

THE DEVELOPMENT OF HUMAN POTENTIAL

Human Resource Development is compatible with sound managerial philosophy. Critical to the success of HRD endeavors is the development of human potential. When an organization succeeds in producing the greatest potential within its employees, unlimited productivity, efficiency and effectiveness is possible.

There's no more powerful motivation than a worthy purpose. When supervisors have the ability to instill inspiration and drive within employees, police professionalism will no longer be a dream; it will soon be reality. HRD specialists can train supervisors how to accomplish exceptional results, both personally and professionally.

Charles Garfield and Brandon Hall are Human Resource Development consultants. Their research and study on human potential and peak performance has won wide acclaim and recognition. Essentially, Garfield and Hall define peak performers as individuals who achieve exceptional results in work that is meaningful to them. They have made an internal commitment to excel. As an organization places a strong emphasis on developing human potential, great things will start to happen.

Creating the desire to achieve a personal peak performance requires that employees constantly strive for goals. The work environment should be filled with excitement and challenge as employees work to be their best. When officers are motivated by what they consider to be a worthy purpose, they will:

1. Be willing to commit themselves to a personal mission.
2. Be willing to take risks in pursuit of their goals.
3. Be willing to accept new challenges.
4. Probably have more motivation than they've ever experienced in their lives.

What's the key to developing and directing this amazing determination to excel? Learning how to assist employees in breaking through to higher levels of personal performance. It's best for both employees and their agency if employees learn how to be more responsible for their own destiny. Irregardless of their current goals or mission, peak performers are filled with an enthusiasm to achieve beyond anything they've accomplished previously.

Anyone can easily learn a basic understanding of the peak performance process by reflecting upon their own previous experiences. A peak performance is any event in one's life when the individual performed at what they perceived to be as an exceptional level. The exceptional performance could have been in athletics, a hobby, on-the-job, or any other endeavor. When reflecting upon a past peak performance, you can mentally relive the exuberance and thrill of the moment of achievement.

Line supervisors can learn a simple exercise that gives employees a solid source of motivation. The exercise involves "leading" employees as they reflect back to their own previous peak performance. It's a simple, yet, very effective motivational tool. Participants are asked to contemplate upon five questions and write a brief synopsis for a later discussion.

1. Describe the concerned accomplishment (one sentence).
2. What motivated you to attempt to accomplish it?
3. What did you learn about yourself from the experience?
4. How did you feel as you were working toward achieving your goal?
5. How did you feel when you accomplished it?

The thrill and exhilaration of dedicating oneself to achieving a goal, then succeeding, usually inspires anyone. Most of the world's greatest achievers have been those who thrived on this sensation of exhilaration and achievement. Their lives were comprised of successive peak performances. Imagine the level of productivity a police department can have when the majority of its employees are motivated to this extent. Even when the topic of their peak performance has nothing to do with law enforcement, officers stay motivated and inspired to do their best in everything.

Obviously, this has been a superficial description of developing human potential through the peak performance process. More extensive information may be found in the text, *Peak Performers: The New Heroes of American Business,* by Charles A. Garfield. The peak performance process is an example of how human resource development can be a sizeable benefit for any law enforcement agency.[32]

Conclusions Regarding Human Resource Development

HRD should become an intrical part of every police organization. Formal recognition and solid commitment from top management must come across loud and clear. The entire staff should be prepared to play an important role. Coaching and support skills can assist supervisors in effectively enhancing a tone of cooperation and teamwork. Developing an atmosphere that promotes ongoing participation and involvement by all employees makes a significant difference in the degree of quality provided.

Human Resource Development helps all employees learn new ways to look at themselves and their job. Personal confidence and a sense of worth will grow, as everyone becomes more attuned to quality and service. Improved teamwork will create enhanced cooperation, sharing ideas and thoughts, depending upon each other and the mutual belief that everyone can contribute to the productivity of the agency.

The principles of an effective HRD program are consistent with the path to professionalism. Agencies travel at various speeds and along different paths. No matter what method is chosen, the way to professionalism always requires a dedication to high ideals and the tenacity to overcome whatever barriers lie ahead.

REFERENCES

1. Harold Koontz and Cyril O'Donnell, *Principles of Management,* McGraw-Hill, New York, N.Y., 1964, pg. 13-14.
2. Warren Bonnis and Burt Nanus, *Leaders,* Harper and Row, New York, N.Y., 1985, pg. 3-6.
3. Harold Koontz and Cyril O'Donnell, *Principles of Management,* McGraw-Hill, New York, N.Y., 1964, pg. 11-16.
4. U.S. Commerce Department, *Statistical Annual of the United States,* U.S. Government Printing Office.
5. Rosabeth Moss Kanter, *The Change Masters,* Simon and Schuster, Inc., New York, N.Y., 1983, pg. 38-41.
6. Rosabeth Moss Kanter, "Work in a New America," *Daedalus; Journal of the American Academy of Arts and Sciences,* 107, Winter 1978, pg. 47-78.
7. Neil Chesanow, *The World-Class Executive,* Westchester Book Composition, Yorktown Heights, N.Y., 1985, pg. 173.
8. Neil Chesanow, *The World-Class Executive,* Westchester Book Composition, Inc., Yorktown Heights, N.Y., 1985, pg. 175-177.
9. Thomas J. Peters and Robert H. Waterman, Jr., *In Search of Excellence,* Warner Books, Inc., New York, N.Y., 1982, pg. 34-39.
10. The Citizens Crime Commission of Philadelphia, *Tokyo: One City Where Crime Doesn't Pay,* Citizens Crime Commision of Philadelphia, Philadelphia, Penn., 1975, pg. 17-19.

11. The Citizens Crime Commission of Philadelphia, *Tokyo: One City Where Crime Doesn't Pay,* Crime Commission of Philadelphia, Philadelphia, Penn., 1975, pg. 17-19.

12. John Naisbitt and Patricia Aburdene, *Re-Inventing the Corporation,* Warner Books, Inc., New York, N.Y., 1985, pg. 227-248.

13. Donald Carter and John Gnagey, "A Japanese Management Technique Applied to Local Policing," *FBI Law Enforcement Bulletin,* Federal Bureau of Investigation, Wash., D.C., May 1985, pg. 21-22.

14. Beverly Geber, "Quality Circles: The Second Generation," *Training,* Lakewood Publications, Inc., Minneapolis, MN., pg. 55-56.

15. Beverly Geber, "Quality Circles: The Second Generation," *Training,* Lakewood Publications, Inc.,

16. Richard Tanner Pascale and Anthony G. Athos, *The Art of Japanese Management,* Simon and Schuster, New York, N.Y., 1981.

17. Neil Chesanow, *The World-Class Executive,* Westchester Book Composition, Yorktown Heights, N.Y., 1985, pg. 174-178.

18. Thomas J. Peters and Robert H. Waterman, Jr., *In Search of Excellence,* Warner, New York, N.Y., 1982, pg. xviii.

19. Thomas J. Peters and Robert H. Waterman, Jr., *In Search of Excellence,* Warner, New York, N.Y., 1982, pg. 207.

20. Maynard M. Gordon, *The Iacocca Management Technique,* Ballantine, New York, N.Y., 1986, pg. 117.

21. Thomas J. Peters and Robert H. Waterman, Jr., *In Search of Excellence,* Warner, New York, N.Y., 1982, pg. 311-312.

22. Thomas J. Peters and Robert H. Waterman, Jr., *In Search of Excellence,* Warner, New York, N.Y., 1982, pg. 318-325.

23. Eugene Benge and John Hickey, *Morale and Motivation,* Franklin Watts, New York, N.Y., 1984, pg. 127-128.

24. Eugene Benge and John Hickey, *Morale and Motivation,* Franklin Watts, New York, N.Y., 1984, pg. 127-141.

25. Barbara A. Williamson and Fred L. Otte, "Assessing the Need for Career Development," *Training and Development Journal,* March 1986, pg. 59-62.

26. Barbara A. Williamson and Fred L. Otte, "Assessing the Need for Career Development," *Training and Development Journal,* March 1986, pg. 60-61.

27. American Society for Training and Development, *Serving the New Corporation,* American Society for Training and Development, Alexandria, VA, 1986, pg. 4-7.

28. America's Society for Training and Development, *Serving the New Corporation,* America's Society for Training and Development, Alexandria, VA, 1986.

29. Leonard Nadler and Garland D. Wiggs, *Managing Human Resource Development,* Jossey-Bass, San Francisco, Calif., 1986, pg. 8-52.

30. Leonard Nadler and Garland D. Wiggs, *Managing Human Resource Development,* Jossey-Bass, San Francisco, Calif., 1986, pg. 202-223.

31. Lenny T. Ralphs and Eric Stephan, "HRD and the Fortune 500," *Training and Development Journal,* October 1986, pg. 69-76.

32. From a speech presented to the 1986 conference, American Society for Training and Development, Region IX, Orlando, Florida, September 1986.

Chapter 5

THE FUTURE

WHETHER you are young or old, male or female and live anywhere across the nation, crime affects your quality of life. The fear of attack results in many cities remaining virtually deserted at night. People don't go for evening strolls anymore. For most of us, the idea of going to bed without locking our door now seems naive. Businesses routinely "mark up" prices due to an anticipated loss from shoplifting and internal theft.

Like it or not, America has surrendered a part of itself to criminals. Society has grown accustomed to crime. The problems are similar whether you live in Tampa, Seattle, Baltimore or Salt Lake. Walking through x-ray machines in airports has come to be expected. The six o'clock news being filled with stories about crime is typical. The fact that most police officers wear bulletproof vests is common knowledge. Submitting to polygraph examinations when applying for many jobs is now commonplace. Providing urine samples will soon be routine for some employees.

The liberty our forefathers and many others died for has been compromised by criminals. The freedom afforded Americans by amendments to the Constitution aren't going to protect a wife or mother as she walks to her car at night in an isolated area. Having homeowner's insurance is little comfort to the family who returns home to find their valuables and family heirlooms missing and their home ransacked.

The extent to which our children may live in fear of crime will depend largely upon the future of law enforcement. Divided, we have little chance of great professional achievement. United, the coordinated efforts of administrators throughout the nation can yield new heights of productivity, unprecedented technological advancements and unlimited progressiveness in the battle against crime. The future is what we make of it. If law enforcement fails to meet challenges ahead, it should blame no one but itself.

POLICE EVOLUTION

Generally, the evolution of the police has followed society's attitudes, and culture. The Texas Rangers were formed in 1835 to fight Indians and outlaws. During the mid 1800's a few larger cities passed ordinances to provide for daytime police officers because night watchmen were lazy and incompetent. The United States Department of Justice, the Secret Service and Internal Revenue Agents were organized during the mid to late 1800's, partially due to the widespread political interference and graft within struggling law enforcement agencies.

Periods of war have had far-reaching affects on police professionalism. A "set back" in qualified manpower occurred during World War II as a result of applicant shortages. The lack of qualified applicants resulted in unqualified and poorly suited individuals entering the ranks of many departments. Even now we live with some of the personnel procedures created during the 1940's. Though a solid relationship exists between the quality of officers hired and the degree of professionalism, police personnel selection still lacks uniformity.

Wars also had a great influence on society's attitude toward local police agencies. The social unrest brought forth by Viet Nam is an example of how an unpopular war can create devastating anti-police feelings among the public. Similar local sentiments may be generated from racial tension, labor disputes or any emotional event.

The 1960's was time when municipal police forces were the recipients of severe criticism. Student unrest exploded in the streets as the nation's colleges protested social conditions and the war in Viet Nam. Civil rights demonstrations and riots were almost common in many major cities. The crime rate skyrocketed. Drug addiction had risen to unprecedented heights. America's police officers were caught ill-equipped, unprepared and untrained. A study conducted by the International Association of Chiefs of Police during the 1960's determined that the average officer had received less than 200 hours of formal training.

The criticism of law enforcement created a strong desire to increase the effectiveness of the police. In 1963, Lyndon Johnson established the Commission on Law Enforcement and Administration of Justice.

Furthermore, the Omnibus Crime and Safe Streets Act, the Law Enforcement Assistance Administration and the Law Enforcement Educational Program were a result of the turbulence and unrest society had thrust upon law enforcement. Evolution through improved technology and education was experienced throughout the 1970's.

Though computerization has quickly become a way of life in most departments, the 1960's experienced a general shift away from technically oriented efforts toward a more community minded, crime prevention focus. Supported by influential citizen groups, crime prevention units and neighborhood watch areas have spread throughout the country. Like most perpetual programs, community relations and crime prevention officers are now finding it extremely difficult to sustain interest and commitment within long established neighborhood watch areas. This, however, does not diminish the success of crime prevention. Community oriented policing has been, relatively, very successful.

The crime rate and subsequent conjecture toward the effectiveness of policing is difficult to measure accurately. Crime rate statistics are frequently inaccurate. Statistical accuracy ranges from excellent to totally inept. Since the exact benefit of crime prevention and other units cannot be determined, the true effectiveness of divisions such as intelligence, crime analysis and crime prevention may only be estimated.

Law enforcement has often met the challenges it has faced. Police departments will always be affected by evolution and change within society. History has proven that one of law enforcement's greatest strengths has been the ability to react in the face of adversity. Society's standards for professionalism are high. The police have yet to meet its greatest challenge.

WHEN COPS GO BAD

To a dedicated officer, reading a newspaper headline such as "police officers indicted during drug probe" is devastating. Every profession has members who violate moral, ethical or professional standards of conduct. Yet, when the individual in question is a police officer the offense seems worse. Perhaps it's because no other occupation is afforded so much authority and responsibility. Society has literally given police officers the right to be a judge, jury and executioner. They also feel the police should safeguard and protect law abiding citizens. They expect high standards and offer little sympathy for ineptness or corruption.

Just as with the general public, good cops don't tolerate internal corruption or ineptness. We would be naive to believe future law enforcement can prevent some officers from "going bad." Yet, past and current levels of graft and corruption cannot be tolerated. Agencies must give no compassion to officers who have yielded to temptation. Following due process, automatic termination for a substantial offense must be standard policy across America. The arrest and prosecution of officers must also be initiated when appropriate.

Examining a department having become infiltrated with graft and corruption offers insight as to how other departments may prevent similar problems. If we are to deserve the status of professionalism, then we must learn from past mistakes and press on to achieve unyielding, higher standards for the future. The future is certain; what we make of it is not.

More than 70 Miami police officers were arrested between 1980 and the end of 1986. Chief Clarence Dickson has written, "paranoia and suspicion has run rampant through the police department and city hall, to the extent that free verbal expression cannot be exchanged without fear that the halls, telephones, desks, walls and offices of everyone who is part of the decision-making process is illegally bugged."

The inside of the Miami Police Department is filled with suspicion and uneasiness. Officers must live with the fact that they neither respect nor trust many fellow officers. Major drug dealing has been conducted by some officers. Others have been charged with murder. The special investigation section has found $150,000 missing from its safe. Several hundred pounds of marijuana is also missing.[1]

The purpose here is not to examine isolated incidences of officers who have gone astray. We must inspect what went wrong with the organization. Further, our inquiry should be taken in the context of constantly seeking what can be learned, to safeguard against similar travesties in the future.

Demoralized, ashamed, sickened, scared, and frustrated are appropriate for how some Miami officers feel. Who's to blame? Certainly the officers having committed unethical, immoral or illegal acts. Yet, what about supervisors who take part in, or allow conversations that demean or ridicule administrators? How about top level managers who conveniently remain unaware of low morale or dissension within the department? Aren't they responsible for taking quick and decisive steps to correct department-wide apathy? Who is responsible for those who are indifferent toward the law enforcement code of ethics? Could administrators be to blame for wide-sweeping internal policies which are blatantly unfair? Could local politicians be guilty of political interference or persuasion that results in demoralizing the rank and file?

The nightmare within the Miami force also involves racial tension. White, black and hispanic officers are openly angry and distrustful of each other. Separate bulletin boards are displayed in the hallways. Various groups allege others have initiated investigations of them. Resentment over hiring practices and promotions have torn fellow officers even further apart.

Responding to public pressures created by two devastating riots in the last ten years, the city has attempted to revolutionize the police department. Depending on who you ask, unprecedented recruitment and affirmative action efforts have been beneficial or harmful. The facts are clear: within two years, the department was transformed from a strong majority of white males, to 60 percent minorities. It increased in size from 650 officers to 1,050.

An agency that was once dominated by white males, suddenly finds they comprise only one third of the force. Two out of five Miami officers are hispanic. Women account for approximately 11 percent of the force. Almost one in five officers are black.[1] Having a majority of officers who are minorities does not mean the agency will be ineffective. What went wrong is the manner of the transformation.

Such staggering changes did not come without a price. Many veteran officers were convinced they stood little chance for promotion. It appeared to them that efforts were being made to hire and promote only minorities. Supervisors at all levels were becoming discouraged by the changes within their department. In turn, newly hired minority officers resented the animosity they felt from senior officers.

In January of 1984, Chief Ken Harms was fired by black city manager, Howard Gary. Like most veteran officers, Chief Harms became frustrated when interdepartmental policies suddenly changed. He was bombarded by white officers who were irate over the number of minorities being promoted. At the same time the city manager demanded he promote more minorities. In a war in which there are no winners, Harms, a good cop, lost.

Herbert Breslow replaced Ken Harms as Chief of Police. Breslow was quick to follow the city manager's recommendations to double his number of top administrators by including more blacks, hispanics and a woman in the top echelon. Several civic leaders and politicians applauded the promotions, feeling the department had finally come close to reaching the "recommended" integrated level of top administration.

Many within the department, however, openly ridiculed and remained disillusioned by the far-reaching promotions.

There was ample reason to be angry over the way promotions were handled. Seven officers were promoted from sergeant to major. In doing so, many lieutenants and captains were totally overlooked. Internal and political contacts appeared to be the overriding credential necessary for these promotions. One of the concerned officers had been a leader in the black benevolent association. Another was a former head of the Fraternal Order of Police. One female officer was the organizer of the women's officer group.[1]

Any officer not understanding what the promotions meant was either naive or very dense. The message was clear. If you were going to get anywhere within the department, it's who you knew that was going to get you there. Loyalty, dedication and hard work are nice, but they didn't help you climb up the ladder of success. Affirmative action, being the right color or sex, playing politics well or having friends in influential places had become the essential ingredient for success.

By January of 1985, Chief Breslow had been fired. Once again, city politicians had forced the Chief's termination. Clarence Dickson, a black, replaced Breslow as the new chief of police. Though many problems have occurred under Dickson's reign, the rank and file generally believe the department's internal problems are not his fault.

One unit that has repeatedly been the focus of criticism is the city of Miami personnel division, which has overseen the department's hiring practices. In all fairness to city hall, the early 1980's was a period of incredible pressure and tension. First, there was the wave of muriel immigrants. This was followed by the Liberty City riots. The riots had been ignited by the acquittal of five white metro officers who were accused of murdering a black man. To make matters worse, Miami continued to experience a very high violent crime rate.

One logical conclusion is that the city needed more police officers. Theoretically, the hiring of more minorities should have helped to sooth racial tensions. Once again, the problem was the way they were hired and promoted.

Though personnel officials claim hiring standards were never lowered, that's difficult to believe, since the force grew from 650 officers to 1,050 within two years. Every experienced chief of police or sheriff knows when you hire less quality officers, there's going to be lower quality performance. The consequences of superficial or indiscriminate hiring practices can be crippling.[1]

The "dark side" of the Miami Police Department is ugly and repulsive. Fellowship and comradeship were replaced with animosity, resentfulness and distrust. Many dedicated officers are marked with the label of corrupt cop by some citizens. Even so, there is no reason the Miami police can't rebuild. A "culture change" must replace distrust with respect and unity. Management must become totally committed to sincere "people management."

What can administrators across the nation learn from examining the experiences of the Miami Police Department? What mistakes made in Miami can be avoided by other departments? Circumstances that contributed to their demise include:

1. The lack of internal training and supervision necessary to instill a high degree of moral and ethical conduct.
2. An exceedingly high number of inexperienced officers.
3. The lack of experienced field training officers.
4. Political interference and manipulation.
5. A level of personnel growth beyond the capability of adequate training and supervision.
6. The failure to sustain high standards of hiring practices.
7. Three chiefs of police in slightly more than three years.
8. A top heavy administration.
9. Four different city managers within four years.

PERCEIVED FUTURE PROBLEMS

The difficulties faced by the chief administrators of the Miami department were considerably greater than most administrators face. Future sheriffs and chiefs will have their share of problems, however. Having an appreciation for potential future problems will assist in finding solutions.

Edward J. Tully is the unit chief, education/communication arts unit, FBI academy, in Quantico, VA. In August of 1985, he surveyed the graduating class of the National Executive Institute to determine their opinions of perceived future problems. They were asked to identify three problems that will be most critical to their agency prior to 1990. The following problem areas were most frequently listed:

A Changing Crime Pattern (Area One)

Crime has an evolutionary tendency. An assortment of sociological influences cause crime to evolve in direct correlation with changes in society.

America has been gradually evolving from a two parent family society to one in which there are an increasing number of single parent homes. The single parenting trend should continue. Studies indicate approximately 30 percent of all children will be in single parent households by 1990.

Additional changes in parenting will also be experienced. There will be a rise in the number of "latchkey" children; those who stay alone after school. Children raised primarily by non-parent relatives will increase. The increase of single parent households will also result in more households living on public welfare. Poverty, violence and a lack of mentally healthy childhood environments may prevail.

The "crime prone" age is usually considered to be fourteen through twenty-five. As the baby boom generation of the 1950's moved into middle age, a significant decline in the number of crime prone citizens occurred. The result has been a general decrease in crime rates throughout the nation.

Though the number of crime prone individuals has decreased, some changing family characteristics have strong negative implications for future policing. There is a belief that many children raised in "broken" households will be living in an environment which furnishes temptation for them to become involved with crime. There may be more opportunities to become associated with individuals and situations conducive to crime. A lack of parental supervision and family togetherness can exist in any family. Yet, parents in a broken home face an uphill battle.

The nature of future crime will require that officers spend more time on domestic related situations like family disturbances, runaways, drug and alcohol abuse, shoplifting, neighborhood quarrels and child abuse. A generation of poverty stricken, single parent raised children may be very susceptible to drug abuse. As such, the police will be faced with an increasing demand for drug enforcement, drug related violence and drug generated property crimes.

Another transformation in crime is being caused by changing technology. New crimes generated by high technology will necessitate the development of advanced and innovative investigative techniques, specialized and highly trained investigators and a financial commitment to the manpower and resources necessary to cope with such demands. Industrial espionage, an assortment of computer offenses, bank and credit card counterfeiting and a new variety of frauds are increasing in frequency.

The Judicial System (Area Two)

At some point, the American system of criminal justice is a source of frustration for virtually all officers. Regardless of rank, or assignment, the system's inadequacies have a way of sometimes seeming unbearable.

Legal restrictions that appear unjust may seemingly result in criminals remaining beyond justice. Prosecution of those arrested must be carried out by an overworked and understaffed prosecutor's office. Overcrowded court dockets cause endless delays and continuances. Plea bargaining continues at a rate that often seems ridiculous. Judges, public defenders and court employees face the same overworked and understaffed working conditions.

Inmate overpopulation will continue to be a serious problem. Overcrowding conditions are going to escalate in severity. Financial resources are not going to alleviate this quickly worsening situation because it's a politically unpopular problem. These conditions will increase the internal difficulties of correctional management and the number of inmates released prior to the end of their sentence.

Personnel Matters (Area Three)

Though often underestimated in value, the personnel division of a police department has always been one of the most critical of all divisions. An agency's commitment to hiring employees of the highest quality should be utmost in the department's overall objectives. Unless an active commitment from the top administration is demonstrated, less than acceptable levels of performance will result, because the standards of employment were not high enough.

Aside from the primary responsibility of hiring qualified and capable officers, an assortment of challenges now face the personnel division. Age, race and sex discrimination will continue to be a concern. Hiring restrictions will be difficult, to say the least.

Standards of conduct and related attitudes already appear to be detrimentally affected by a decline in society's values. The desire for quick and superficial gratification, increasing materialism and a decline in values, morals and ethics cause many internal personnel problems.

Examinations administered to applicants will be under great scrutiny and challenge. Entrance examinations, fitness tests, medical examinations, polygraph examinations, drug abuse and psychological tests will continue to be questioned as to their validity and fairness. Developing and implementing examinations based upon a job task analysis and job relatedness is already essential. Hiring the best person for the job isn't as easy as it used to be. In all likelihood, the future will mean even more difficulty.

Some future problems lie in the areas of drug testing. For the good of society, drug abuse can't be tolerated in some occupations. Law enforcement is obviously such an endeavor. Officers must remain mentally alert, morally sound and capable of setting a standard for all to follow. Certainly a "drug free" body is a legitimate personnel qualification for any department. Though few would disagree with this premise, an assortment of issues and concerns should be addressed before adopting a procedure. The two basic concerns are that it provides a reasonable safeguard for society and furnishes appropriate safeguards for individual rights.

The current drug testing controversy generally focuses on two areas: pre-employment drug screening and drug testing of current employees. Many interrelated questions arise regarding the implementing of these controversial and litigious procedures. The following issues are frequently raised.

1. Can pre-employment drug tests be conducted without pre-notification to concerned applicants?
2. How will law enforcement agencies develop a testing vehicle which adequately provides for the identification of and protection from the unintentional consumption of drugs, as well as the validity and reliability of the drug screen itself?
3. How will urine tests account for the fact they do not provide any information regarding the recentness of use, how the person was exposed to the drug, or whether the illicit drug was ingested at all?
4. Can drug tests of current employees be conducted at random, without prior notification?
5. How will the test be designed to protect the unintentional drug consumer from termination based on a positive result?
6. What type of procedural safeguards are necessary to ensure the evidentiary credibility of the evidence?
7. What will employers do when an employee's drug test indicates positive?
8. What constitutional rights do concerned employees have?
9. How will employers ensure employees that a reputation or career will not be destroyed by a false or inaccurate reading of a drug test?[2]

The mandatory use of urine analysis has been challenged in two forms: the circuit court and the public employees relations committee. The court has placed strict limitations on government's ability to maintain a drug screening policy. Courts have held governments must have evidence constituting reasonable suspicion an employee is using a controlled substance before it can require a urine test. This prevents administrators from routinely ordering a test as a condition of continued employment. Employees can refuse a test unless the agency can establish some evidence of drug abuse. In 1985, the city of Miami ordered three officers to submit to a urine analysis. When the officers refused, they were terminated. Their union bargaining agent appeared before the public employee's relation commission alleging the terminations were forbidden under the current labor contract.

PERC ruled against the city of Miami. The commission, however, did not decide that requiring urine analysis testing for government workers was illegal. It held this particular type of examination, as a condition of continued employment, should be a mandatory subject of bargaining.

The city claimed, under terms of the concerned contract, the union had waived its right to bargain over the imposition of urine analysis testing. The commission declared there had not been a clear and unmistakable waiver of the union's right to negotiate a change in the city's policy regarding drug testing. The discipline was found to be illegal and the officers were ordered reinstated. The concerned legal cite is Fraternal Order of Police, Miami Lodge 20 vs. City of Miami, case number CA-85-041, December 11, 1985.

The hearing officer for the Miami case held the city had not previously required this type of testing under current contract. Furthermore, it was a change in the terms and conditions of employment. Since the urine analysis had an adverse impact on employees, the change could not be implemented unless it was a result of collective bargaining.

Most labor contracts have clauses regarding the rights of management. The Miami case, for now, holds that all contracts with public employers in Florida will be interpreted differently than in the past. Officers will retain all bargaining rights unless each waiver within the contract is clear and definite. The waiver of bargaining rights should be demonstrated through language which confers the authority to change the terms and conditions of employment upon the employer.[3]

Funding (Area Four)

The need for adequate funding has always been worrisome for police executives. The past ten to fifteen years, however, has brought forth ever increasing reasons for concern. Now, more than ever, police administrators must be proficient at all phases of financing. Many factors are having substantial influence on the financial operations of law enforcement. These include:

1. The sporadic and unpredictable nature of the economy.
2. The constant flight of the middle class to the suburbs.
3. The relocation of many industries from northern industrial areas to southern states.
4. The declining revenue base of older industrial cities.
5. A substantially decreased amount of federal funding for law enforcement agencies at the local level.
6. A shift from federal to state and local responsibility for numerous social ills.[4]

The fiscal realities of contemporary America demand the police increase productivity, reduce spending and find new sources of revenue: a task easier said than done. Many funding sources have disappeared. Raising taxes is politically less prudent than in the past. Top local government officials are, and will, expect high levels of fiscal competence.

JOBS AND GROWTH

American industry has served our nation well for a very long time. Since the industrial base is evolving to a new information/electronic economy, many practical considerations must be understood. John Naisbitt, in his nationwide, number one best-seller, *Megatrends,* contends we now live in a new and different economy. One in which both new problems and great opportunities exist. One key to successful leadership of any organization is the ability to appreciate how these facets of society should be appropriately dealt with.

The United States is restructuring itself. Many interrelated components of our economic lifestyle indirectly and directly effect the daily operations of government. Naisbitt alleges the critical restructurings are:

1. The growth of many older industrial cities of the North have ceased as people move to the South and West regions of the United States.
2. The United States can no longer function as though it is an isolated, self-sufficient, national economic system; we must acknowledge the U.S.A. is merely an important part of a global economy.
3. We are moving toward a society of new technology that has a compensatory human response.
4. The United States has shifted from an industrial society to one based on the creation and distribution of information.
5. Americans are restructuring their lives from receiving a great deal of institutional help to being more self-reliant.

6. We, as a group of people, are abandoning our dependence on hierarchical structures in favor of more informal ones.
7. Our former network of representative democracy has become obsolete in an era of instantaneously shared information.
8. Our society is transforming from an emphasis on short-term considerations and rewards, to viewing things in much longer time frames.
9. We are moving from a narrow either/or society with a limited number of personal choices, to an exploding, freewheeling, multiple-option society.
10. All types and sizes of organizations are rediscovering the ability to act with great innovation and achieve results from the participatory form of management.[5]

Many of these trends will have a direct effect upon law enforcement of the future. Perhaps the most obvious is a shift from an industrial base to one of high technology/information. The massive use of computers has already enabled increased efficiency within many divisions of a police department.

While their effect is less obvious, other trends are also having considerable influence. The shift of economic and population growth from North to South has noticeable consequences. Employment, personal income, education, life-styles and housing have been altered as a result. These and other changes create reactions in the rest of society.

Changing growth rates play havoc with local governments. Many areas of the South are overwhelmed by population increases. Demands upon governmental entities have brought forth strained abilities for service. The North, however, is frequently riddled with the opposite problem. Municipal governments are finding their cities being abandoned by residents. The result upon the police is crippling:

"New York City has reduced its police force by 21 percent, its firefighters by 7 percent, and its sanitation workers by 16 percent since 1975. But New York's subway and transit system is in the worst shape of all: already running a 170 million deficit, the Metropolitan Transit Authority figures it needs 14 billion for repairs over the next ten years. New York City itself needs thirty to forty billion dollars over the next ten years for long-delayed repairs to capital facilities.

The Chicago Transit Authority is just barely making its payroll each week. Meanwhile, the city's school system must come up with a busing plan — extremely difficult in such a segregated city — and the twenty-five million needed to implement it.

The city of Detroit is virtually bankrupt, having already cut services substantially. The city has laid off some thousand police officers and must cut the city work force by some 12,000 workers. We are fresh out of miracles," says Mayor Coleman Young.[6]

The National Planning Association, a non-profit research organization, reports that service jobs are having the largest percentage of increases in net growth across the country. Furthermore, the growth having been concentrated in the Southwest and the West now appears to be more "balanced" across the United States.

The association also notes most of the growth is located in metropolitan areas. Three hundred and seventeen selected metropolitan areas are projected to account for 86 percent of the next 43 million additional jobs. The following table concerns top metropolitan areas for job growth from the years 1985 through 2010. Specifically, areas having the biggest anticipated annual job increases are depicted.

AREAS WITH BIGGEST ANNUAL JOB INCREASES

1.	Naples, Florida	1.6 percent
2.	Fort Myers, Florida	1.5
3.	Fort Pierce, Florida	1.5
4.	Las Vegas, Nevada	1.5
5.	Reno, Nevada	1.5
6.	Orlando, Florida	1.4
7.	Atlantic City, New Jersey	1.4
8.	West Palm Beach/Boca Raton/ Delray Beach, Florida	1.4
9.	Fort Lauderdale/Hollywood/ Pompano Beach, Florida	1.4
10.	Gainesville, Florida	1.4
	(percentages rounded off)	

Source: National Planning Association

Societal Generalities — The preceding conversation regarding growth, funding and economic influences paints a fairly dark picture. Rightfully so; the early 1980's was not an easy period for police departments. After more than a decade of substantial federal aid and budgetary expansion, funding for law enforcement failed to increase and in many cases, dwindled substantially.

All departments should prepare for continued financial restraints. Many agencies have already experienced the brunt realities of poor economic times. Working with equipment that is outdated, unsafe or in need of repair is one result. A decrease in overtime pay, fewer or no promotions and having to lay off employees are others. Drastic budget cuts are felt in all divisions. A reduction or total elimination of many programs and units have been the solution in some departments.

Law enforcement has been slow to implement the proven management practices of the private sector. When faced with financial difficulties, agencies typically respond by trying to balance their budgets through marginal adjustments and operating procedures and expenditures. The aforementioned examples are typical of short-term adjustments that are taken in hope of not experiencing a loss of visible operating effectiveness.

When additional revenue decreases occur, administrators usually find they are no longer capable of carrying out fundamental responsibilities. Rather than problem solving from a long-term perspective, temporary and superficial solutions are sought. Eventually, quick answers "catch up" with an agency if increased funding is not restored. Serious losses in professionalism and service usually occur.

One generality that is difficult to accept by most police professionals, yet soundly documented, is that policing has little impact on the nature or extent of crime. Certainly there are aspects of crime prevention that have impacted crime levels. Neighborhood watch groups, various crime prevention seminars and some internal programs do make a difference. The difference is small in comparison to the overall crime level, however. The fact remains that policing, in general, is still reactive in nature.

Policing in America is very decentralized. Every agency at the local level has a strong degree of independence pertaining to it's structure and internal operations. Decentralization is taken to such extremes that agencies frequently have little or no knowledge of intelligence known by neighboring agencies. Isolation also occurs internally. Some officers have no concept of the responsibilities or problems officers in other divisions have. As sad as it may be, this amount of independence and isolation is consistent with America's tendency for isolation among its citizenry.

Law enforcement is shaped by society's socioeconomic characteristics. Changes within society have direct impact on the police. Analyzing and projecting future sociological trends provides great assistance for predicting the future of policing.

JAPANESE POLICE/FUTURE IMPLICATIONS FOR AMERICA

The police of Japan are considered by many to be the most efficient in the world. Their reputation for excellence stems from an ability to accomplish more, with less resources. Great insight for American police can be gained from Japanese law enforcement.

Subculture—The police of Japan enjoy a substantially higher social status than their counterparts in the United States. The primary reason is that the Japanese police culture is based on dedication. A very high degree of respect exists through solid values and a unity of purpose.

Initial training involves not only technical skills, but thoroughly socialized officers in the police way of life. The first objective of recruit training is usually "complete life guidance," which may be defined as the development of a just and cheerful character and harmonious good sense.

Becoming a Japanese officer usually means a lifetime career commitment. Officers are quickly taught the following motto:

> Warm and human solidarity
> Kind, cheerful reception
> Strong, correct enforcement[7]

The Japanese are extremely proficient at instilling high degrees of loyalty, commitment and dedication. Lifetime employment and a family oriented atmosphere are promoted. A profile of excellence and quality performance has been the result.

America would benefit enormously from developing a culture of trust and teamwork. It is unrealistic to think in short-range terms, however. The reason is that it cannot occur without changing the current management style. Changing habits, tradition and attitudes requires overwhelming management commitment.

Achieving the management transformation will be a long, tedious process. The results will be more than acceptable to most administrators, yet the missing ingredient for success is usually the total, active commitment from high administrative levels. The commitment should be so strong that actions will speak louder than words.

Recruitment—The lack of "lateral entry" is widely acknowledged and accepted by American law enforcement. Initial employment is typically restricted to patrolman status. No consideration is given to hiring officers for "higher" positions, irregardless of the individual's education, past experience or specialized abilities. The basis for continuing this personnel practice is tradition, for it certainly isn't logic or sound reasoning. Such a policy prevents the most qualified and capable personnel from assuming their most appropriate positions in an agency. It is nothing more than an illogical custom.

The Japanese, on the other hand, recruit for entry into two distinct levels: patrolman and assistant inspector. As with America, patrolman may rise through the ranks to whatever level their ability takes them.

Employment directly to the rank of assistant inspector is offered to attract personnel with the education levels and intellectual ability necessary for staffing high administrative positions. The assistant inspector position requires applicants have a four year college degree and pass an advanced civil service examination.[8]

If the future of law enforcement in the United States is to be guided by efficient and qualified administrators, they must have the knowledge, skills and abilities to perform their responsibilities accordingly. Though not impossible, it's senseless to believe the most capable individuals for high administrative positions will always be officers who've risen through the ranks with only superficial in-service or advanced training. Compare this to a policy which requires administrators to possess a business related four year college degree. While a college degree does not ensure superb managerial performance, it does indicate that individuals have the knowledge necessary to be excellent managers. Ensuring that managers apply that knowledge effectively is the job of the chief administrator.

Supervisory Training

Another reason for Japan's effectiveness is their commitment to supervisory training. Upon promotion to sergeant, an office automatically attends a three month in-service training program. Newly promoted assistant inspectors must attend a six month managerial course. When an officer is appointed to the position of inspector he attends a full year's training course at the National Police College in Tokyo. Though Japan is only the geographic size of California and has slightly fewer officers per capita than in the United States, every year approximately ten thousand officers undergo supervisory training.[9]

Employee Benefits/Labor Relations — There are less material benefits for police officers in Japan than in America. When considering only salary, Japan's is substantially lower. Japanese officers, however, receive extensive fringe benefits that American officers must pay for. As an example, approximately 55 percent of all officers live in furnished housing which is provided for little or no cost. The Tokyo Metropolitan Police Department make available housing for families at a cost of less than a tenth of the current market price.[10]

Japanese officers may belong to two cooperative associations which provide supplementary retirement, health and disability benefits. The associations also offer low cost loans and an assortment of retail goods at reduced prices. Excellent motel and vacation resort areas are available at extremely low rates through the associations.

All police officers are provided with free hospitalization and medical care. Greatly reduced prices for common necessities like laundry, restaurants, retail stores and medical supplies are furnished. When loans are necessary for purchasing items such as furniture for newylwed officers, police departments provide them.

Japan does not have police labor unions or other organizations that represent officers to police management. The welfare section of police headquarters manages most working condition related matters which would be of concern to a police union in the United States. The "mutual benefit association" oversees police, hospitals, motels and housing complexes. Administered by the police headquarters, it's financially supported through deductions from all officers' paychecks.[11]

Japanese police do not have labor unions because they do not need them. America would be wise to learn from the way Japan treats their officers. American labor organizations are analogous to band-aids, they merely cover up the infection. They do not cure the wound.

Unions have not developed in Japan because officers are treated better than they are in America. Whereas Japanese officers have more pride and dedication, their American counterparts frequently feel animosity or distrust toward their employer.

Once again, the solution for the American police is a change in management style. A change that will not come quickly. The initial step is to have chief administrators with the courage and foresight to persist in efforts to develop an atmosphere of teamwork, cooperation and dedication.

TRANSFERRING JAPANESE MANAGEMENT TO AMERICA

To ask if Japanese management can be transferred to American law enforcement agencies is an unfair question. History can document administrators who have had the courage to implement new managerial philosophies. Some of these leaders may be the same administrators who realize the Japanese style of management has existed within the United States for a long time. The truth is that a few American quality control experts are largely responsible for transforming Japan's reputation for manufacturing from the brunt of jokes, decades ago, to that of world dominance.

Several major corporations had people-oriented management prior to World War II. IBM and the Hewlett-Packard Company are good examples. These and other exceedingly well run organizations treat their employees as an extremely valuable resource.

Most of corporate America has been very bad at people management. Movies like *9 to 5* and *Take This Job and Shove It* express bitter feelings. The strength of the Japanese lies within their people management. Understanding that America has also had shining examples of people management, we should address how law enforcement agencies can successfully adapt participatory, people oriented management.

Because the police have also had a bureaucratic, strict, authoritarian style of management doesn't mean the police cannot change. It is all the more reason they should change. People oriented management doesn't infer a lack of discipline. Discipline, when needed, is dealt with in an appropriate fashion. Participatory management doesn't profess supervisors no longer have the final decision. Just the contrary, quality circles are a valuable fact finding tool. Division heads still make the final decisions, after quality circle determines the facts.

The key ingredients to Japan's people management include devotion, "bottoms up" management, dedication, commitment, lifelong employment and harmony among employees. Thus, the keys to success are nothing more than caring about those you work with. In doing so, everyone has the opportunity to make a difference. This, in itself, is an invaluable motivator.

SOCIAL AND TECHNOLOGICAL FORECAST

Only the future will tell whether policing meets the challenges of the future. If they are to be truly professional, administrators must transform their organizations so the opportunities of tomorrow will be seized to their greatest potential.

When an organization develops this new management philosophy, unexpected opportunities will appear. Employees will be eager to stay informed of the latest developments, trends and technologies of the future. Officers will thirst for the knowledge needed to develop ideas and generate innovative thinking for the good of the agency.

The future offers nearly unlimited opportunities. When innovative thinking is encouraged and employees are no longer afraid to take risks, departments will have the strength needed to create a better tomorrow.

Effective organizations encourage employees to think of the future. They disseminate information which stimulates progressive thinking and rewards those who strive for improvement.

The World Future Society is a highly respected, non-profit organization that provides unbiased information relating to the future. The information concerns new developments, possibilities, forecasts and trends. The society believes that sharing such information with individuals, businesses and governments will assist in creating a better future for everyone. Some of the latest forecasts from the World Future Society include:

> **Forecast #1** — By the year 2000, the typical car will be comprised of plastic and will last approximately 22 years.
>
> **Forecast #2** — By 1995, most employees will be working 32 hours per week. Many will be preparing for future careers. Though work weeks will be shorter, school weeks will be increasing in length.
>
> **Forecast #3** — Fifty-two percent of the world's population by the year 2000 will reside in urban centers. By the end of the 21st century the percentage may rise to 90 percent.
>
> **Forecast #4** — Scientists will have succeeded in synthesizing the human growth hormone. Mexico City already has a population of 17 million people. By the year 2000 the population of Mexico City should rise to 28 million people.
>
> **Forecast #5** — Vehicle accidents in the future may be reduced to only 10 percent of current levels as the result of microcomputing technology.
>
> **Forecast #6** — Largely due to the destruction of tropical forests, plant and animal species may be disappearing at a rate of 10 thousand per year, by the 1990's.
>
> **Forecast #7** — Within the next decade, the American economy will generate four to five trillion dollars in new capital assets that encompass the next generation of applied technology. However, unless current financing techniques are altered, many small businesses may find the availability of credit more restricted than today.[12]

Crimes of the Future — Crime rates rose 300 to 400 percent in the 1960's. They leveled off in the 1970's and have dropped in the 1980's. This is not to infer that America does not have a severe crime problem. Most of today's crimes are not what the general public perceives them to be. Contrary to a popular belief, violent crime is not what victimizes most Americans. White-collar crime has become much more commonplace.

"Violent crime comprises only 10 percent of major crime in the United States and the rate of violence is dropping. While street crime costs us about 4 billion dollars a year, frauds, embezzlements, forgeries, counterfeiting and other white-collar crimes costs between 40 billion and 200 billion a year," states criminologist-sociologist, Georgette Bennett. Bennett is the author of the book, *Crimewarps: The Future of Crime in America.* Recognized as an expert in the field of American crime research, her predictions include:

1. White-collar crime will increase; violent crime will decrease.
2. Future crime will be committed by today's stereotype victims — the elderly and females.
3. Though teenage related crime will decrease, what remains will be more violent.
4. The computer will be known as the greatest crime tool of all time.
5. A demographic crime shift from city to suburban and even rural areas will occur.[13]

A CHANGE OF ATTITUDES

If police professionalism is achieved, a change of attitudes must occur. The traditional American "mind-set" of supervising employees is frequently synonymous with ordering, demanding and making subordinates work. The best managerial attitude is one of explaining, helping, leading and coaching fellow workers to improved performance.

The business community seems to accept change easier than law enforcement. Perhaps it's because they have more incentive to do so — profit.

In 1965, the Harvard Business Revenue surveyed business executives to determine how they felt about women in the work place. The same survey was conducted in 1985. The differences are astounding:

- In 1965 approximately 75 percent of men surveyed stated they would be uncomfortable with a woman supervisor. In 1985 the figure was 53 percent.
- In 1965 more than 60 percent of men surveyed and half of the women believed "the business community will never wholeheartedly accept women." In 1985 these percentages had dropped to 20 percent of the men and 40 percent of the women.
- In 1965 50 percent of men and 25 percent of women advised women were temperamentally unfit to be executives. Only 18 percent of the men and 5 percent of women still hold these views in 1985.[14]

The Disney Way — No better example of how organizations may successfully enhance attitudes can be found than in Walt Disney World.

Valerie Oberle and Rick Johnson of the Disney University at Walt Disney World are masters at inducing positive change. Every new employee of Disney World attends an extremely well developed orientation program.

The initial phase of orientation occurs in the "tradition room" of Walt Disney World. It is here that new employees are greeted and the perpetual evolution of Disney philosophy begins. Employees are quickly asked to complete a brief historical quiz on Disney traditions. Following completion of the quiz, they discover the answers to every question surrounded them in the form of large colorful pictures portraying historical Disney events.

The Disney approach to people management is simple: their highest priority is a Disney employee. Walt Disney once said, "You can design, create and build the most beautiful place in the world, but it takes people to make the difference." That philosophy is inbred in all new employees. The importance of teamwork, a sense of humor and always doing your best are ingrained whenever possible. Whether someone has been a Disney employee for a day or a decade, everyone does his best to make the organization a family.

Disney management is convinced their employees' quality of work life directly affects the overall productivity of the organization. They document facts to support their opinion. The overall turnover rate at Disney World in 1985 was 24 percent. For salaried employees it was 16 percent. These percentages are extremely low. For the service industry, they are virtually unheard of.[15]

THE FUTURE OF CORPORATE TRAINING

Certainly the innovation and progressiveness of Disney is not typical in the corporate world. Their future is particularly bright because they've had the foresight and wisdom to step ahead of their counterparts.

The first national survey of corporate training and development managers was conducted in 1986. It encompassed telephone interviews with 750 training and development managers. One hundred and eighty-seven questions regarding training philosophies and practices were posed. Highlights of the outcome include:

- Approximately 80 percent of the responding companies budget specific funds for annual training. Approximately half of the companies increase their training budgets for 1986.

- The training topics most mentioned by industry trainers include supervisory skills, employee orientation and management development.
- Training managers do not usually have "exclusive" control of their training budgets.
- More supervisors and staff members are sent to outside training seminars than other employees.
- Almost 50 percent of those surveyed advised they use some phase of computers within their training program.
- Approximately 50 percent of those surveyed advised they formally evaluate their internal training programs.[16]

As demonstrated by the preceding survey results, industrial training is not perfect. Like law enforcement, the future holds many challenges. Unlike law enforcement, corporate trainers tend to appreciate the value of employee development. Contrary to police agencies, human resource development units are not rare. The future is particularly encouraging for many industries because they've already begun to reap the benefits of innovation and teamwork.

Professional Certification—Certification is the process through which a professional organization recognizes the competence of individual practitioners. Its primary purpose is to identify and improve professional competencies. Competencies should be performance oriented and reflect the skill of a professional. The individual's title and rank or academic degree must be irrelevant.

Additional benefits of professional certification include:

- It promotes professionalism.
- It provides incentive for individuals to remain in a given profession.
- It enhances the prestige of a profession.
- It allows for individual recognition among peers.
- It assists in identifying both competent and incompetent practitioners.
- It provides job security and discourages internal transfers.

Law enforcement associations should work to establish professional certification programs. These procedures are applicable to all levels of law enforcement. They may be applied to specializations such as instructors, canine officers, crime prevention officers, detectives, trainers and supervisors. The benefits of certification can be derived by the police whenever a certification process is implemented.

PROFESSIONAL REGULATION

An important element of professionalism is law enforcement's ability to regulate itself. Examining the successes and failures of the legal, accounting and medicine professions will furnish insight as to how the police should proceed.

Self-Regulation of Lawyers — America has 700,000 lawyers for a population of 240 million. One hundred thousand lawyers have begun practicing law in the past five years. In the District of Columbia, one in every twenty-three people is a lawyer.[17]

The American Bar Association has always encouraged local bar associations to establish regulating/disciplinary committees. In this way, lawyers are afforded the right to regulate themselves through the judgement of their peers. Committees typically deal with matters of alleged unethical conduct.

On the state level, state supreme courts may have the sole authority to investigate or prosecute lawyers. They may also delegate their authority to state bar associations, which investigate and prosecute lawyers, but the court decides matters regarding discipline.

Controversy has now arisen among American Bar Association members. The issue is whether the right to regulate and discipline attorneys should continue to be handled by lawyers. Some members of the bar association believe "non-lawyers" would more aggressively discipline the profession.[18] The question of whether lawyers should continue to be self-regulated will haunt the profession as long as self-regulation exists.

Accounting Self-Regulation — Like other professions, the professional reputation and the ability to self-regulate accountants have recently come under fire. Accountants are now attempting to convince the public their self-regulatory process is effective. CPAs are generally considered to be responsible for protecting the investments of unknowing citizens.

The idea of self-regulation for CPA firms began in the early 1970's. Like all professions, issues regarding the development and implementation of this type of program generates a lot of controversy. At the time, the American Institute of Certified Public Accountants didn't have jurisdiction over CPA firms. In 1977, the institute created a separate division that now has theoretical jurisdiction.

CPA firms throughout the nation were asked to voluntarily join the division. In doing so, the firms undergo a peer review process. Firms seeking membership must meet thirteen independent requirements.

The use of peer evaluations, extensive membership requirements and the peer review of CPA practices have greatly improved the quality of the accounting profession.

The success of self-regulation in the accounting profession lies in the thoroughness of the regulatory process. Only firms which have sound quality control practices and adhere to strict rules will pass the close examination. The following facts illustrate how thorough the process is:

FACT: Member firms must submit to the peer review every three years. During the first series of reviews, 86 percent of the CPA firms passed the review. This percentage climbed to 94 percent during the second series. The increase was primarily the result of remedial actions demanded during the initial reviews.

FACT: Even though a firm passes the review process, weaknesses will be reported. Letters explaining the firm's weaknesses are forwarded. Upon receipt of the letters the firms must respond in writing.

FACT: Approximately 1600 CPA firms have voluntarily submitted to the quality control system by undergoing the peer review process.

FACT: These firms employ approximately 50 percent of all certified public accountants in public practice.

FACT: Firms which do not "pass" the peer review process must take immediate corrective action. The corrective action may include having audit reports checked prior to issuance by auditors from other firms prior to issuance. The firms may agree to an accelerated peer review process, or to a revisit by the peer review team to ensure their quality has improved.[19]

Self-regulation of the accounting profession is slightly more than one decade old. As with any transformation of this magnitude, there have been good times and bad. Initial resistance was met and overcome. Many similarities exist between accounting's experiences and law enforcement's newly implemented accreditation program. John W. Zick, deputy senior partner of Price Waterhouse, summarized the status of self-regulation in the accounting profession as he delivered a speech to a conference of accountants on April 25, 1985.

The accounting profession has accomplished what no other profession has yet attempted. We have taken aggressive steps to regulate ourselves and at the same time improve the quality of accounting and auditing practices.

But because we covet the public trust, more may be expected of us. We have and we will respond by being willing to walk the extra mile.

Our self-regulatory process works quite well within its design perimeter. The process is educational, remedial and quality-enhancing.

Does that mean no changes can or should be made? — No. We need to move our self-regulatory process forward, improve and enhance its credibility and — at the same time — do our best to build a better public understanding of the role of CPAs. We have created a self-regulatory system that works. While it may not be perfect, I believe its light-years ahead of other professions — and I am proud of it.

The American Medical Association — The American Medical Association is America's largest association of physicians. It has recently committed itself to strengthen efforts to rid the profession of physicians guilty of misconduct or incompetence.

Like the police, the medical profession is riddled with the belief that physicians engage in a brotherhood of silence to protect fellow physicians. The AMA has met these allegations "head-on" by developing a program that encourages doctors to report incompetent colleagues. Dr. John Coury of Port Huron, Michigan was inaugurated as the AMA president in June of 1986. During his address at the association's annual meeting, Coury stated, "If we are to prove that this is not true, we must become even more committed to taking forceful action against physicians who are sore spots in our profession — the incompetent, the arrogant, the fraudulent, the impaired, the greedy. And we have taken a major step at this meeting."

Acknowledging that physicians who speak out against dishonest or incompetent colleagues may be sued, the association pledged to provide legal and financial assistance if the need arises. In addition, the AMA will now review the credentials of its 280,000 members and expel any physicians who have lost their licenses.

The effectiveness of the program has been enhanced by the use of a computer registry. This allows for easy inquiry of past disciplinary actions of physicians who may by applying for employment to medical staffs across the country.[20]

Future Perspectives

The endeavors of law, accounting, and medicine have and continue to earn the status of a profession. The preceding summaries of their efforts are vivid examples of how law enforcement may approach similar problems in the future.

The national accreditation process has taken great strides in achieving standardization. The continued growth of a centralized body of policies all agencies may strive for holds enormous potential for the future.

Like the medical profession, Florida has taken the lead in establishing an effective method of decertification, after a "due process" identifies dishonest officers. Decertification means the concerned officer will no longer be certified to be an officer anywhere in the state. This provides a great service to other agencies which might have unknowingly hired the officer.

Like highly recognized professions, law enforcement uses state government bodies to regulate the licensing or certification of officers. Unlike the professions of law, accounting or medicine, the minimum education standard is substantially lower. In addition, the concerned professions have major non-union organizations which promote professionalism while providing assistance to individual members.

Certainly, the Fraternal Order of Police and the Police Benevolent Association promote professionalism. Yet, they are also associated with unionism by the public. The International Association of Chiefs of Police remains a very progressive and worthwhile organization. Even so, it is not structured for all police officers to become active members. I.A.C.P. membership is approximately 15,000. There are almost 40,000 agencies in America. The future must yield a single, unified organization to represent and unify all police officers.

CORRECTIONS AND PROFESSIONALISM

A wide array of instability has prompted renewed interest in professionalism for correctional facilities during the last two decades. A series of severe riots generated concern both internally and among the general public. The phenomena of rights for inmates has also emerged. Serious overcrowding and mandatory release of inmates has created enormous controversy.

Examining efforts to professionalize the field of corrections offers valuable input for future consideration. Enlightenment can be gained by studying a progressive correctional facility which has sought to professionalize.

The scope of criminal justice professionalism has gradually evolved during the century. In the early 1900's, it was synonymous with ridding the nation of police corruption and unjust political influence. The 60's and 70's on the other hand, was a period when professionalism meant the furthering of training, education and technology. The experience of the unnamed correctional facility substantiates that the focus of achieving professionalism should be on transforming the managerial style from bureaucratic to participatory/people oriented.

Like many facets of the judicial system, efforts to professionalize corrections have been limited to increasing the training/educational level and providing new equipment. This is evident in the following case study. For ease of understanding and clarity, only this case will be presented. The study, however, is consistent with an ever increasing body of research on the implementation of organizational reforms.[21]

Believing an educated staff was the answer to it's quest for professionalism, the correctional facility generally ignored management style. Substantial problems within the organization were not addressed. Supervisory commitment to quality and effectiveness was very low. Appropriate strategies for implementing reforms were never developed.

After experiencing many serious problems in the mid 1970's, the governor of this state called for the reform of the state prison system. The prison's budget was significantly expanded in 1979. A new director was retained and a promise for reform was declared.

Major reorganization efforts were quickly begun by the new director. The implementation of more humane inmate treatment, establishing new internal policies and the centralization of administrative control highlighted the reorganization. The termination or reassignment of many senior supervisory officers was carried out.

The agency's desire for professionalism was also demonstrated by a $3000 annual employee raise. In-service training was increased to a mandatory sixty hours per year, per correction officer. The American Correctional Association's accreditation standards dealing with job descriptions were met when the organization incorporated new counseling and supervision of inmate programs. The agency granted preference to applicants with a four year degree, strongly encouraged the furtherence of college education and increased the minimum education hiring requirement from a high school diploma to fifteen hours of college credit.

Obstacles to Professionalism — Though the correctional facility implemented a wide assortment of measures and programs to promote professionalism, crucial factors were overlooked. Increasing the salary level or educational requirements alone, will not produce professionalism. The correctional agency failed in their effort because their organization lacked vital ingredients for successful organizational change.

Obstacles to effective implementation of change can be overcome if the plan for change includes the necessary elements. Rosabeth Moss

Canter, a highly acclaimed author and management consultant, promotes these elements in her landmark book, *The Change Masters*.

Element 1 — A Culture of Pride. All levels of supervision must work together to encourage pride within the organization. The achievements of all employees should be recognized and rewarded. An internal newsletter, plaques, certificates, trophies, paid time off, monetary rewards and the personal appreciation of an immediate supervisor are crucial to instilling the sense of pride and "ownership."

Element 2 — Tools For Innovative Problem Solving. The organization must establish vehicles through which innovative and progressive ideas may be tried. Such tools will stimulate the highest quality of performance capable by all levels of employees. Examples include cross-level problem-solving teams, performance appraisals which reward innovation and progressive action, along with the implementation of problem-solving techniques.

Element 3 — Improving Lateral Communications. Teamwork, cooperation and harmony are evident in effective organizations. They are absent in agencies which are stagnate and inefficient. It is crucial employees from different areas who share interrelated responsibilities, communicate effectively and harmoniously. Any action that brings employees together to communicate problems, responsibilities and opportunities for improvement is a wise investment.

Element 4 — No Unnecessary Layers of Hierarchy. Having too many "layers" of hierarchy prevents employees from having access to the resources they need for innovation and progression. The authority to make decisions must be transferred downward. In addition, information which assists in bringing forth increased productiveness from *all* levels of the agency must be shared freely. There should be little or no obstacles to the resources necessary for productive undertakings. This does not mean there shouldn't be proper documentation of resource allocation.

Element 5 — Sharing Information. The importance of disseminating information throughout an organization can't be overemphasized. In addition to being necessary for making productive decisions, it's vital to an atmosphere of teamwork and cooperation. Its absence creates a feeling of secretiveness, distrust, fragmentation and the lack of cooperation. Employees at lower levels must be given the chance to contribute to the organization's future, prior to decisions being made at the top. Informative newsletters, employee group discussions and quality improvement teams are ideally suited.[22]

The aforementioned correctional facility concentrated on several important changes, yet the elements Rosabeth Moss Canter stresses were not emphasized. In failing to address these issues, any organization, no matter how noble their intent, dooms itself to failure. Failing to combine staff upgrading with all encompassing organizational reforms caused the correctional institute to unknowingly increase the frustrations of employees.

The experiences encountered in this case study are very common. If we are to be successful in our struggle to overcome inefficiency and stagnation, then deep organizational problems must be dealt with. Most of these problems involve anti-productive styles of management.

Specifically, the correctional institution provided little or no training that focused on developing an atmosphere of pride and teamwork. "Bottoms up" management that encourages employee participation was not implemented. Staff members were frustrated, confused and felt threatened. The lack of harmony and teamwork was evident as a supervisor spoke about a change of titles in the organization:

> I told you that I really think this change in job title from 'correctional security officer' to 'correctional service officer' is a step backward for the officer. It makes us sound like servants or wet nurses. It takes away our authority and respect (supervisor).
> The administrative guidelines were developed by people who never worked in a cell block. We are getting a lot of officers in here with degrees and no common sense. We need more experienced personnel, not necessarily more educated ones (supervisor).[23]

There are common misgivings concerning the improvement of an organization's intra-structures. Though the intended improvements initiated by the administration of the correctional facility were important, it was what the administration neglected to do which is of more importance. The failure to ensure a transformation to a people-oriented/participatory management style guaranteed failure.

PLANNING FOR THE FUTURE

In 1973, the national advisory committee on criminal justice and goals established specific goals and standards for the future development of law enforcement in America. Standard 5.4 dealt with agency and jurisdictional planning. Clearly, all the recommendations of the national advisory committee have not been met. Yet it is important we appreciate the wisdom and foresight of their collective reasoning. Let it serve as an example in establishing the importance of planning throughout all law enforcement agencies. The committee, in part, recommended the following:

All police agencies should immediately identify the types of planning necessary for effective operations. Specific responsibility for research and development, along with agency and jurisdictional planning should be assigned.

All agencies having seventy-five or more personnel should establish a planning unit, staffed with a minimum of one full time employee who's responsibilities include intra-agency administrative planning and coordination of all planning activities.

Every agency organized into subdivisions should delineate divisional planning responsibilities and provide personnel accordingly.

Agencies having fewer than seventy-five personnel should assign responsibility for administrative planning and coordination of planning activities within the agency. If the magnitude of planning activities justify a full time employee, one should be assigned. If such activities do not, the responsibilities for planning should be assigned to an employee with related duties.

All agencies should assign the responsibility for maintaining a close interagency planning relationship. Agencies within the same area or frequently deal with each other should be active in frequent mutual planning sessions.

Every law enforcement agency should participate in cooperative planning with government organizations in the same jurisdiction. Planning for the future, in areas of mutual concern, is critical among all governmental agencies in the same jurisdiction. The responsibility for ensuring every agency is represented in planning associations must be carried out.[24]

Effective planning is an essential ingredient for the future. "Management by crisis" is much too frequently relied upon. The opportunities that lay ahead cannot be taken advantage of without anticipating future trends and developments. The absence of sound planning can be politically devastating, financially crippling and managerially disruptive.

Effective planning involves the assessment of organizational weaknesses and strengths, establishing objectives and goals, identifying potential trends, collecting needed information, analyzing data and ensuring developed plans are implemented. Once again, the police can learn a great deal from the corporate world. Some agencies have already done so, and are remarkably efficient at planning. Administrators who've yet to recognize the importance of planning may seek the assistance of these agencies to learn how and why they developed planning divisions.

One infrequently addressed, yet, potentially disastrous influence upon police planning is fragmentation of the criminal justice system. Law enforcement can't plan efficiently from within a vacuum. The police have both direct and indirect effects on other components of the system, just as they affect law enforcement.

The major units of the American judicial system are the police, courts and corrections. Planners of tomorrow should view each as part of a whole system. Those concerned with the future must further the integration of the individual components into a unified and productive system.

Long-range planning should account for the realism and practicality of daily life. The general public can furnish input useful to the planning process. We can only be prepared to take advantage of what the future has to offer if we efficiently plan for it.

COMMUNICATION

Theoretically, the word communication is defined as a process by which information is exchanged between individuals through a common system of symbols, signs or behavior.[25] Realistically, it simply means exchanging information. Law enforcement has not communicated well in the past. Any veteran officer can cite examples of problems that were created because one division or unit did not know what the other was doing. Classic examples are often experienced when detectives investigating a series of offenses learn other detectives have been investigating offenses with identical methods of operations.

The lack of good communication can also cause distrust and bitterness. Good communicating travels not only up and down in an organization, but laterally throughout divisions, as well. The responsibility for effective communicating lies with all levels of management. If the top administration does not actively encourage open communicating, communication will be lacking. Easily established vehicles like an internal newsletter, ensuring frequent staff meetings that disseminate information and the promoting fellowship will work wonders.

On a county-wide basis, examples of good and bad communication are prevalent. Due to necessity, investigative divisions through the community now frequently meet to exchange investigative intelligence. Detectives have developed an appreciation for exchanging information and ideas. They have learned the hard way, that failing to do so almost certainly means inefficiency.

Many state and nationwide associations have worked very hard to improve communications throughout law enforcement. Organizations such as the *Police Foundation, International Association of Chiefs of Police, Fra-*

ternal Order of Police, Police Benevolent Association and the *United States Department of Justice* should be supported and encouraged to continue their efforts. Commitment to a purpose can mean different things to different people. If law enforcement is to reach its fullest potential, administrators must set an example for their staff by freely sharing information and ideas. Becoming an active member of professional associations is a good way to improve communication at all levels.

PROFESSIONAL ORGANIZATIONS

To a large degree, the extent to which the police have achieved professionalism is directly contributable to a handful of police organizations. How receptive rank and file officers are to the guidance provided by them will influence how professional we become. The receptiveness of officers depends greatly upon their immediate supervisors. Once again, it is leadership that will decide our future.

Without question, the *Federal Bureau of Investigation* has been a driving force for professionalism of the police. Led by J. Edgar Hoover, the *Bureau's* relentless desire for improvement and excellence has been a model for all to follow. Exceedingly high standards of employment sets the FBI apart from the majority of law enforcement. Their assistance with training to local agencies has been invaluable to many departments. In addition, the benefits of the National Academy are both everlasting and far-reaching.

The International Association of Chiefs of Police continues to mold the shape of law enforcement. It exists as a prime example of the good that can be accomplished when groups of dedicated individuals merge their efforts for a worthy cause. As a volunteer organization, the IACP offers an assortment of worthwhile committees upon which members may serve. While the committees generate a great deal of work for members, they benefit officers throughout the nation. The "all encompassing" nature of the *IACP* strives tirelessly for professionalism through innovative and progressive leadership.

A tradition of excellence is proudly proclaimed by the *Southern Police Institute*. Founded at the University of Louisville more than thirty-five years ago, the Institute has graduated thousands of police administrators. Its pursuit of excellence and unyielding demand for high academic standards are consistent with the highest ideals of law enforcement. As a result, the Institute enjoys a reputation for providing the highest quality training.

The late Dr. Joseph D. Lohman, former sheriff of Cook County, Illinois and Dean, School of Criminology, University of California, first suggested organizing the Southern Police Institute. David A. McCandless, former director of public safety, Louisville, Kentucky, carried out Dr. Lohman's suggestion in 1949.

Initially, the *Institute* offered three, twelve week courses for 25 officers. As time passed the faculty expanded, it's financial base grew and the curriculum intensified. The Institute became the first school of its type in America to offer college credit for in-service police education.

Currently, the nucleus of the Southern Police Institute is a twelve week administrative officers course. Enrollment for the 1985-86 academic year included 117 administrative officer course graduates, 213 graduates of on-campus seminars and 511 graduates of off-campus seminars. It issued 1,931 credit hours and 2,752 continuing educational units during the year.[26] The *Southern Police Institute* will continue to be a leader because it has grown from a tradition of excellence.

The *National Criminal Justice Reference Service* is an essential tool for any progressive law enforcement manager. It enables quick retrieval and dissemination of current and available information.

As the primary research agency of the U.S. Department of Justice, the National Institute of Justice was created for the purpose of providing realistic and practical solutions to the daily problems of police management. Through a toll-free telephone number, any interested party can solicit from a seemingly endless reservoir of criminal justice related information. NCJRS is able to provide a centralized national information clearinghouse through its computerized data base. Law enforcement officers may, at their convenience, receive access to the data base by phoning the toll-free number 800-851-3420. When calling, ask for a specialist with expertise in the field of law enforcement, community crime prevention or corrections. The *National Criminal Justice Reference Service* provides the expertise needed for the challenges of tomorrow.[27]

The mission of the *Police Foundation* is to promote improvement and innovation in America policing, and to help the police in their quest to reduce crime and disorder. Founded in 1970 through the efforts of many of the nation's most prominent police executives, the *Foundation* was initially funded through 30 million dollars provided by the *Ford Foundation*. The funds were used to assist several police departments in progressive research.

The *Foundation* has provided more than useful research for the police. It has nurtured the initiative of many agencies and led them to reach new heights in developing and implementing practical improvements. It continues to contribute a great deal to law enforcement. Patrick Murphy, former president of the *Foundation,* summarizes areas of concentration he believes should be addressed by the police of tomorrow:

1. The restriction of deadly force must be increased.
2. The use of civilians within police agencies should be increased.
3. Raising the level of college education must become a high priority.
4. Neighborhood policing should be further developed and expanded.
5. Agencies should continue to raise levels of minority employment.[28]

THE FUTURE OF CORPORATE MANAGEMENT

Corporate America is facing a crucial transformation. It must continue to transform the social and economic environment of the 1960's to better methods of management. Due to the competitive nature of private enterprise, industries which do not have participatory/people-oriented management will be forced to do so. Companies will rely more upon the individuals within their organization. Managers throughout the nation will learn the primary difference between innovative and stagnate companies is the degree to which participation by employees is induced.

America is in the midst of a productivity crisis. At best, our current struggle to improve effectiveness, productivity and quality of work is fragmented and sporadic. We, as a nation, have a long way to go.

Some corporations, however, have been managed in a very effective manner. Organizations like Honeywell, Disney, Apple and Hewlett-Packard have been shining stars in the darkness. These corporations are people-oriented because those who founded them appreciated the value of having dedicated and innovative employees. A tradition of treating every employee well is a high priority for these organizations. As potential managers rose through the ranks, this same management philosophy was instilled within them.

Leaders of Tomorrow. A leader is an individual whom others follow. There are different types of leaders. Some are born leaders—they possess charisma. Others have had leadership bestowed upon them by assuming a position of management within an organization. Unlike charismatic leaders, they usually do not retain their leadership after leaving a particular position.

Regardless of the type of leader, good leaders have certain qualities:

- They have the ability to inspire exceptional performance.
- They are able to generalize facts from data and form useful policies.
- Leaders convey extreme confidence. Further, they instill the same kind of confidence in their followers.
- Finally, a leader is an individual who assures continuity of leadership. Leaders of industry are aware of their responsibility to ensure management succession. Those who succeed current leaders must meet or succeed these high standards.[29]

Leaders of tomorrow must appreciate the significance of a good organizational climate — an atmosphere where teamwork and cooperation prevail and errors are embraced. Risk taking, innovation, cooperation and harmony are actively promoted.

Tomorrow's leaders should have the ability to lead their organization through the transformation — one in which outdated, ineffective management is replaced with leaders who act as a coach, counselor and inspirer. Future success requires that administrators have unique qualities and skills. Their capabilities must emerge from an appreciation for the complexities of changing a management culture. Administrators will be called upon to do more than manage their organization, they must lead it.

Effective leaders must possess qualities which enable them to effectively transform their organization. Noel Tichy and Mary Anne Devanna, in their recent text, *The Transformational Leader*, present the characteristics of transformational leaders:

They identify themselves as change agents. Their personal and professional image must signify they have the means to successfully carry out the transformation. They are professional managers who have grown into transformational leaders.

They are courageous individuals. Those who are capable of taking necessary risks, able to take a stand for what they believe in and to withstand the pressures of "change."

They are value driven. They must possess a deep and abiding set of values that are exhibited in their own behavior. "Setting an example" must be a constant ingredient in their own management style.

They believe in people. Powerful, yet sensitive to others, transformational leaders are not dictators. They possess the ability to motivate and inspire the best from those around them. They deeply believe an effective leader is also a coach, counselor and cheerleader.

They are lifelong learners. They sincerely feel life is a never ending process of education and self-improvement. They encourage others to always broaden their perspectives and knowledge.

They are visionaries. Transformational leaders are capable of translating dreams and images into realistic, practical realities. They are fully aware of how their actions will affect others throughout their organization. They strive for endless betterment.

They possess the ability to deal with ambiguity, complexity and uncertainty. Such leaders can manage the multifaceted ramifications of a rapidly changing world. Problem solving, turning sound theory into practical reality, and never ending improvement, are crucial qualities.[30]

Developing Leadership. The concept of leadership means many things to different people. There are literally hundreds of definitions of leadership. Obviously, it is fair to say that leadership is complex and multifaceted.

Leadership is exercised differently in the business world than within government. This is because there is a vast difference in restraints, regulations and the environment of the two sectors. To a varying degree, the more restrictive policies of government are a "necessary evil" due to the expenditure of taxes. As a result, increased bureaucracy creates more inefficiency.

It is not unusual for leadership seminars and development programs to be sponsored by local governments. Those attending sometimes take diagnostic tests to determine their "current suitability" for leadership. The idea is that supervisors with unsuitable management styles must be identified before they or anyone can change their style to one more compatible. The quality of these courses vary with the abilities of particular instructors. Many offer training consistent with people-oriented management. This, of course, is contrary to most police supervision instruction which still reinforces the demoralizing authoritarian/bureaucratic approach.

Leadership theories are varied and plentiful. Chief administrators can use their imagination to find ways of merging people-oriented consultation and instruction into daily operations. All staff meetings should include an aspect of management style as an agenda item. Open, lateral communication, among supervisors is crucial, particularly during transformation. There should be several topics of these discussions: the present status, future considerations and how they as leaders should play a role in the transformation.

Law enforcement administrators are responsible for ensuring that the actions of every staff member is based on an active commitment. Commitment must be more than merely agreeing with the new leadership philosophy. It requires that each staff member talk, act and live people-management. It also means that supervisors under their command do the same. It relies upon interaction and communication at all levels of the organization. Though supervisors have always been expected to encourage good communication, this role is now much more important.

Michael LeBoeuf, Ph.D., in his book, *The Greatest Management Principle in the World*, does an excellent job of summarizing how supervisors may improve the quality and overall performance of employees through an improved system of communications and rewards. The following table summarizes LeBoeuf's management principle:

STRATEGY: WHAT TO REWARD

Reward	*Instead of*	*With*
1. Solid Solutions	1. Quick fixes	1. Money
2. Risk taking	2. Risk avoiding	2. Recognition
3. Applied creativity	3. Mindless conformity	3. Time off
4. Decisive action	4. Paralysis by analysis	4. A piece of the action
5. Smart work	5. Busy work	5. Favorite work
6. Simplification	6. Needless complication	6. Advancement
7. Quietly effective	7. Squeaking joints	7. Freedom
8. Quality work	8. Fast work	8. Personal growth
9. Loyalty	9. Turnover	9. Fun
10. Working together	10. Working against	10. Prizes

ACTION: WHO AND HOW TO REWARD

Manage Others	*Manage Your Boss*	*Manage Yourself*
1. Choose the results you want.	1. Inventory strengths and weaknesses.	1. Choose a new habit.
2. Identify the behavior needed.	2. Build on the strengths.	2. Choose a fitting reward.
3. Decide on the proper rewards.	3. Decide how you want to change your boss's behavior.	3. Practice the habit for three straight weeks.
4. Use the power feedback.	4. Reward your boss for signs of positive change.	4. Give yourself the reward, enjoy success and choose a new habit.[31]

Remember to always reward with positive, encouraging communications. Rewards should be immediate, spontaneous, warm and sincere.

CHARACTERISTICS OF FUTURE ORGANIZATIONS

Outdated and ineffective management has to change if organizations are to compete in the future. In addition to falling behind in the competitive work of profit, employees are now changing as well. They view things differently than in the past. Studies indicate that over half of society's young people now have college aspirations. They've begun to question rigid authoritarian bureaucracies. There's even a trend toward being less motivated by financial rewards and more inspired by the way they are treated. They want the chance to be involved, the opportunity to make a difference and appropriate recognition when they've done so.

Besides future management being people and participatory oriented, it will also be nurturing. Administrators can accelerate the development of leaders by delegating rather than telling. All employees should be encouraged to create ideas and develop them. Even though some ideas may not be fruitful, the fact that they took the initiative to try must be recognized and rewarded.

Supervisors will be rewarded for results rather than for their number of subordinates. Employees won't be penalized for making mistakes which resulted from risk taking. The central headquarters staff will be very small in number. Administrative hierarchy, in the terms which we now know it, will disappear. Many management positions will be dissolved and replaced by groups of employees who remain self-managed through a team-participatory, decision-making process.

Organizations will find large centralized staffs are unable to respond quickly. As a result, the structure of successful future organizations will be flat, flexible and decentralized. Decentralization gives individual units and divisions the leeway to act quickly to changes without having to clear decisions through the usual bureaucratic, time-consuming methods.[32]

Innovation means being creative or introducing something new. It's a necessity for any profession. The future will be of little significance without it.

Historically, law enforcement has had varied success with innovation. Many beneficial forms of technology have been integrated into police operations while remaining cost-effective. The police, however, continue to use large amounts of funding on high technology such as with the use of helicopters, or with an assortment of electronic systems in the expectation that these will provide a significant improvement.

Without doubt, technology has proven itself time and time again. Yet, it's crucial that decisions to purchase new equipment are scrutinized to ensure these are fully applicable to the concerned objective. There has been a tendency to view technology as a "cure-all" when problems arise.

This is not intended to infer technology hasn't been extremely beneficial for law enforcement. On the contrary, the benefits of technological advancement can be seen in virtually every community across the nation. The danger is that policing has ignored another type of innovation — people.

In terms of innovation, the future is what we make of it. If the police fail to meet the challenges ahead, they have no one to blame but themselves. We must grasp the vision we can become, then be relentless in our pursuit of it.

THE FLORIDA INNOVATION GROUP

The Florida Innovation Group is an organization of Florida cities, counties, and private companies joined together for the purpose of expanding the use of science and technology in local governments. It serves as a glowing model of how governments may learn from the corporate world.

Its mission is to work together in bringing about cost reductions, service improvements and productivity increases to the public and private sectors, through the implementation of technologies, processes and ideas. The principal thrust of FIG's effort is the identification and transfer of technology to local governments from private industry.

FIG is a non-profit, tax exempt corporation with the ability to enter into contracts with public and private entities for the purpose of science and technology research, transfers and applications in local government. A steering committee of local government and private sector representatives give policy guidance, management direction, program review and evaluation.

Subcommittees deal with specific issues such as public/private cooperative efforts, venture capital investment in programs of interest to local government, and specific FIG projects. A staff of professional, experienced administrators manage day-to-day operations. Unfortunately, few states have a similar organization.

Approximately fifty local governments and corporations throughout Florida are members of FIG. Members are obligated to:

- Provide policy and program and direction to FIG staff.
- Inform technological needs.
- Identify innovations to be shared.
- Serve as evaluation site for new technologies.
- Identify local companies with innovative products and/or programs.
- Join in cooperative projects with local governments and the private sector.
- Have staff persons participate in seminars, workshops, and information exchange.

There are a variety of benefits to being a member of the Florida Innovation Group; they include:

- Technology transfer.
- Technology inventory.
- Access to national data banks.
- Cooperative projects in areas of common interest.
- Seminars and workshops for management personnel, elected officials and functional specialists.
- Newsletters and bulletins regarding innovation projects, cost savings and product test results.
- Private sector linkages for technology development, cooperative ventures, application of resources to local government issues, product testing and product development.
- State university research centers to assist with research of local government technology and local government issues.
- Federal agency research of test results and products for local governments.

Source: The Florida Innovation Group

INNOVATION OF THE FUTURE

America has evolved into three distinctive eras since the turn of the century: agricultural, industrial and the current information and technology era. By the year 2000, the nation will present many new challenges to law enforcement. Hopefully, technology will advance fast enough to be of assistance in finding long-term solutions. When administrators take advantage of all technology has to offer, they will be better prepared to provide levels of service likened to the highest ideals of our forefathers.

Training—A high standard of training is a basic prerequisite for attaining professionalism in any endeavor. Training has been terribly neglected throughout the history of law enforcement. Until recently, it received little support or commitment by administrators. Even today there are chiefs who claim a commitment to training, yet, don't provide nearly enough manpower or financial resources to carry out the training function. Some states have no mandatory in-service training requirements. Very few states have organized associations through which training officers may improve their abilities, skills and knowledge.

We still view training in terms of a particular number of hours afforded each officer. Officers are ordered to a classroom where they receive a lecture for a specific period of time. Frequently, there is no examination to indicate whether any learning occurred. If a test is given, more likely than not a pretest was not conducted to allow an accurate determination of the degree of learning.

Lesson plans are usually absent. Intended learning outcomes (behavioral objectives) are rarely written. Documentation may or may not be adequate. Training officers and internal instructors usually don't receive adequate training themselves.

Law enforcement **must** keep pace with training related technological advancements. It should continue to reach for new heights of technological expertise. Society will not consider the police to be professional without it. Those undergoing training must be held accountable to specific, measureable learning outcomes. Agencies, on the other hand, must be responsible for furnishing training that is based on sound curriculum design. That which is cost effective, self-paced, individualized, appropriately documented and effectively presented.

A sound investment in technology will permit the police to increase the effectiveness of training and reduce the overall expenses associated with it. Additionally, the age-old dilemma of training versus the need for manpower "on the street" may be resolved.

Interactive video and computer assisted training systems will be of tremendous assistance to the police of tomorrow. They may also be of great benefit to current police training. Effectively applied technology provides the following training advantages:

1. Automatic standardization is accomplished both in terms of quality and content.
2. Highly efficient documentation is achieved with a minimum of manpower.
3. The individualism afforded by self-paced instruction allows officers to learn at a speed most appropriate for them. This enables those who perform at a quicker level to continue instead of being "held back" by slower students.

4. The expense of computer assisted and interactive video training will be lessened for many departments, since they have already acquired component parts such as computers or video cassette recorder systems.

5. Individual instruction furnishes perpetual training without the necessity of requiring large groups of officers to be taken away from their normal duties.

6. Since most agencies now pay overtime salaries, the perpetual, individual training permitted by technology may substantially reduce overtime expense.

7. Computer assisted instruction provides an ongoing, accumulative training record of every employee.

8. Computer assisted instruction can easily identify areas where additional training is needed.

9. Video training furnishes a level of realism and understanding not possible through lecture instruction.

By the turn of the century, some equipment now thought of as "science fiction devices" may be standard issue for police officers. As technology increases its amazingly rapid development, many aspects of criminal detection, identification and apprehension will be enhanced. Though some avenues of highly sophisticated technology are available now, most remain too expensive for widespread use by the police.

Teleconferencing is a good example of technology already widely used throughout the business community. Conferences involving people located thousands of miles apart are held over closed circuit television. Frequently, the use of satellites is instrumental in this form of communication. When teleconferencing becomes available for the police, the ability for executives and specialized experts to communicate effectively will be of great benefit.

Holograph photography will allow the rapid transmission of three dimensional photographs over great distances. The ability already exists, but, high cost prevents it from being widely used. The future will probably find holograph technology replacing "mug shots." Holograph photographs, besides being three dimensional, display the subject's height, weight and other physical attributes from all sides.

Computers will find their way into most homes by the year 2000. As a result, citizens may be able to request police assistance through their computer terminals. Police communications personnel will instantly determine the closest available unit through the use of computer assisted dispatching systems. This is already in use within some jurisdictions.

Officers responding to a call will have mobile computer terminals in their vehicles. Enormous local, state and federal data banks will let officers determine an assortment of information pertaining to the individuals involved in the call to which they are responding.

Cyanoacrylate adhesives (super glues) and the use of lasers have become very helpful in developing latents which would have remained undetected. Prints from skin, cloth and porous materials, along with very old ones can now be identified.

The benefits realized from computers will spread throughout any agency. Some detective divisions already have the ability to search and identify latent fingerprints, maintain M.O. files, develop huge amounts of investigative intelligence and retrieve specific investigative records. Automated fingerprint identification systems technology has revolutionized law enforcement's ability to apprehend criminals and solve crime.

The central records division will also reap great benefits from advanced computerization. Most reports will be automatically entered into the computer system as patrol officers use mobile terminals. Word processing operators can enter administrative and investigative information that's been tape recorded. Some agencies may have computers capable of storing information through voice interpretation, eliminating the need for a typist.

Communications systems, will be far advanced from those currently in use. The mobile computer terminals now being used in some police vehicles may be supplemented by hand-held terminals. Portable video cameras will be mounted on the dash board of vehicles to assist in documenting drunk drivers and recording "routine" traffic stops. The cameras will be easily detached for video taping crime scenes and witness statements.

Additional forms of technology may include "wristwatch" computers and information banks, jet "backpack" flight machines and a variety of non-lethal weaponry. Highly sophisticated forensic crime scene technology and extremely sensitive surveillance equipment will be commonplace. Robotics may be used for barricaded building entry, bomb disposal and community relation purposes.

A Day in the Life..., James R. Metts, the first sheriff in America to earn a doctoral degree, does an excellent job of portraying a day in the life of a future police officer in his article, "A Police Officer's Day in 2001: A Futuristic Scenario." The following is an edited version.

Officer Brett Railey, of the Any Town Police Department, is currently assigned to the evening shift. Since roll call was eliminated long ago in favor of teleconferencing via home view phones of officers, there is no need for him to travel to the main headquarters.

Roll call teleconferences are generally the only contact officers have with headquarters. They usually work out of their homes or one of the various substations of the city. Many calls can be handled by view phones. Officers report to headquarters through computer terminals at their substation. Some even have computer terminals interfaced with their own personal computers.

When all officers on the shift dial the department, the shift lieutenant starts roll call through the teleconference view phone. On this particular day, the majority of discussion concerns a series of recent armed robberies.

Officer Railey is assigned to a special robbery surveillance detail. He drives his department issued propane-powered, three wheeled vehicle to the substation to pick up an undercover vehicle.

The patrol division's vehicle fleet consists of an assortment of three wheeled vehicles, mopeds, helicopters, surveillance vehicles and patrol cars. What's now considered a patrol car is rarely used for routine patrol duties. In fact, they are rapidly becoming obsolete except in a few isolated areas.

Brett welcomed the "change of pace" as he had recently been assigned to monitor the numerous closed circuit television and display screens at the substation. Though monitoring permits officers to "patrol" an entire area without leaving headquarters, Brett looked forward to being on the street again. The electronic monitoring of business and residential areas comprise a major portion of the agency's prevention and apprehension efforts.

As Officer Railey sat in his police vehicle, he reviewed photographs and pertinent information concerning the robbery suspects through his vehicle's computerized telescreen.

A short time after noon, Brett noticed two men, who generally fit the suspects' descriptions, enter the bank. He telephoned bank security with his cellular phone. A plainclothes bank security officer watched the suspects who left without incident after making a brief transaction. As the men were leaving, photographs taken with the bank teller's photomonitor were transferred to Officer Railey's viewphone for comparison with the department's computer memory photograph of each suspect. The photographic comparison identified both suspects as those wanted for the previous bank robberies. After having begun surveilling the suspects from his vehicle, Officer Railey radioed for helicopter assistance.

Within moments the police helicopter had the suspect's vehicle in sight. A few minutes later, with the helicopter shouting commands from above and Officer Railey directly behind, the suspects pulled over. Both were arrested and transported to the county jail.

A few hours later, Railey claimed his special bonus time for participating in the surveillance arrest and left work early. An in-service training class was scheduled at main headquarters but he was able to view it on his home viewphone. He participated in the examination by punching in the answers on his home computer and having them transferred to headquarters.

In a few moments his own computer printed out a score for the test. Brett did well because he had been studying the subject — criminal law — through a home viewphone/computer course offered by a local university.[33]

COMMUNITY INVOLVEMENT

Innovation and progressiveness occur in forms other than technology. While innovation, in terms of community involvement, may not appear initially to be progressive, to a large extent the degree of professionalism depends on how much success law enforcement attains within their community.

The importance of positive community involvement should not be underestimated. Officers who have poor public relations will never be considered "professional" by their own citizens.

Future public involvement, as well as prioritizing services, must evolve around the fact that the police spend a relatively small part of their time handling crime related matters. Remember, the majority of responses by officers deal with calls for service rather than crime. Settling disputes, generally maintaining order, assisting with matters of health or well-being and providing information comprise most calls.

Administrators must realize officers view their purpose as fighting crime rather than public service. Because of this, more emphasis should be directed toward community involvement. Law enforcement can receive a great deal of assistance through effective community involvement programs. Recent examples of creative and innovative community involvement programs can be found throughout the nation.

- Extensive foot patrol programs.
- Assistance to crime victims.
- A police community newsletter.
- Spouse abuse programs.
- Departmental volunteer assistance programs.
- Drug abuse prevention.
- Programs designed to increase officer/citizen contacts.[34]

CONSOLIDATION

The benefits and drawbacks of police consolidation have been debated for years. Many executives are being forced to take a closer examination because of demands for greater efficiency at less cost. Increasing financial restraints, political influence and citizen pressure have already caused many communities to merge police services.

Some states now have county-wide law enforcement agencies. In other areas, agencies have consolidated to form regional departments. In addition, there are almost three hundred metropolitan areas throughout America. These areas are likely communities for consolidation.

More common than the total consolidation of police are partial consolidations of support functions like training, communications or record divisions. Larger departments frequently contract to provide these services to smaller surrounding agencies. Partial consolidation is a way to substantially increase effectiveness and to lower expense, while ensuring the overall independence of each agency.

Critics of consolidation argue that creating large departments will mean the loss of personal contact within their communities. As a result, citizen willingness to assist and cooperate with the police will decline. In reality, however, this is simply not true. Poor citizen contact occurs in small and large departments. As demonstrated by the national police force in Japan, community relations can be extremely good even for a national police agency.

The main reason consolidation efforts are thwarted is that chief administrators fall victim to their own human nature. Many don't want to give up their own particular reign of power. Call it "petty jealousy" or a touch of self-centeredness, administrators must rise above their own self-interest for the good of all who wear a badge.

Though slow in developing, the consolidation of law enforcement will continue its spread throughout the nation. As it does, America will move closer to having a nationally managed police force. Contrary to the illogical criticism of skeptics, it will prove to be of great benefit. Citizens will receive more productivity, efficiency and professionalism.

THE PATH TO PROFESSIONALISM

Attorneys and physicians provide services that usually go unquestioned by their clientele. An assumption of professionalism exists before individuals ever walk into their office. Police officers, on the other hand, don't enjoy the luxury of working in an atmosphere of blind faith. If officers are candid with themselves, they will admit they don't yet deserve this luxury. Should officers go to college for eight years, the public would have more confidence in their actions.

The benefits from professionalism will come in accordance with the degree to which it is attained. In conclusion, the following accomplishments may act as a road map to professionalism:

1. First, officers at all levels must exhibit **professional attitudes and conduct.** A positive, professional attitude by individual officers is essential for society to accept them as professionals. Officers who are driven by high esteem, pride and sound moral values will have no problem in sustaining conduct consistent with the highest ideals of a profession. When any single officer "goes bad" the entire community loses a degree of trust in the department. The nation should have a standardized decertification process.

2. **Professionalism must be instilled** and reinforced throughout an officer's entire career. Law enforcement fails to establish sincere respect within officers, for its tradition, purpose and value. The police academy, in-service training and daily reinforcement by immediate supervisors are logical opportunities for ingraining and maintaining values like loyalty, dedication, service to others, respect and pride in one's self and agency.

3. **Standards of employment** must be raised and adhered to if society can accept the police as professionals. Maintaining high standards of employment is, of course, much easier said than done. Some administrators argue this belief is naive and unrealistic since our salaries and benefits are substantially lower than generally accepted professions. The irony of such logic is that justification for improved salaries and benefits may only be substantiated when law enforcement earns these benefits, as demonstrated by raising standards of employment or education.

4. A high **education level** is a fundamental prerequisite for recognition of professionalism. Chiefs and sheriffs should immediately move to impose a two or four year college degree hiring requirement. Initially, the sacrifice will be great. Higher standards of employment will mean a smaller recruitment "pool" from which recruiting agencies have to choose. The sacrifice, however, will be a wise investment in the long run, because educated officers really are better prepared to perform their duties.

5. **Training must be enhanced** for professionalism to become a reality. Historically, police training has been terribly neglected. The advent of innovative technology has resulted in marked improvements, however. Nationwide standardization of in-service training is non-existent. Generally accepted prerequisites for effective training, such as mandatory lesson plans, pretests, posttests, establishing goals and objectives, curriculum design and thorough documentation are sporadic at best.

6. A law enforcement **code of ethics** is already established, but, it doesn't play an important role in the daily lives of officers. Unlike Japan, perhaps the most effective police force in the world, American officers don't receive regular reinforcement on the importance of the code of ethical conduct.

7. A significant change in **management style** must occur for the police to keep pace with the efficiency of other organizations. Currently, most departments have bureaucratic/paramilitary management. Overwhelming evidence indicates a participatory/people-oriented style of management yields much higher levels of quality performance and effectiveness.

8. An increased emphasis on **human resource development** must take place. The most valuable resource in any organization is its members. Law enforcement neglects to fully appreciate or develop the abilities of police personnel at any level.

9. **Improved career development** must also merge. Many agencies have no formal career development function. As such, they are missing a tremendous opportunity for improvement.

10. **Lateral entry** is a way of life in the corporate world. Successful businesses seek the best person, wherever he or she might be. Law enforcement exists in the dark ages when it comes to ensuring the most qualified and proficient individual is placed in a particular position. Many business organizations would go bankrupt if they operated this way.

11. **Labor unions** have no place in a professional police department. They exist for the betterment of individuals within the union. Their fundamental purpose is not to improve the organization. As such, they act as a band-aid, failing to address the real problems and issues. If American law enforcement successfully addresses the real issues, such as a management style change, there will be no need for unions.

12. **Civil Service,** like labor unions, isn't needed where there's professionalism. The police officers bill of rights, internal grievance

procedures and people-oriented management are more than capable of ensuring fair treatment. Often, civil service simply acts to protect the inept. It is frequently a major obstacle to necessary administrative discipline. Unjust protection of the unproductive and apathetic can lead to a stagnant organization.

13. Without strong and harmonious **community relations,** police departments won't be recognized as professional. The significance of community support will be appreciated when agencies fully understand their role as community servant. It's certainly possible to be a public servant and a professional. Examples are hospital physicians and the ministry.

14. Having the most beneficial **utilization of manpower** is critical to reaching maximum efficiency. The future must include increased use of civilian community service officers, selecting the right person for every position, effective manpower allocation of all patrol officers and less anti-productive bureaucracy.

15. **Consolidation** should continue to spread throughout the nation. It will be recognized as an effective means of improving efficiency at reduced costs and a solid stepping-stone to professionalism.

16. Little **standardization** presently exists within law enforcement. This must change for proficiency of services to occur. State and national organizations must take more of a lead in this regard.

17. The national **accreditation** process should be viewed as the vehicle to be used in establishing nationwide standardization and improvement. Agencies that refuse to acknowledge the wisdom of accreditation will eventually be forced to become accredited by community pressure and civil liability.

18. How the police perceive their own **role in society** is critical to future change. Currently, most officers envision their role as that of a "crime fighter." Actually, they are highly specialized public servants more than crime fighters.

19. **Enhancing the organizational climate** within police departments is necessary to achieve a high level of productivity. When a pleasant working environment doesn't exist, employees usually have low levels of morale and pride. The absence of pride equals an absence of quality.

20. **Technological innovation** must continue its progressive nature. The police have done well in taking advantage of the benefits technology has to offer.

21. More emphasis should be placed on **planning and research** in the future. Though law enforcement has undergone tremendous

change in the last two decades, it has been slow to prepare for the future. Many agencies don't have anyone responsible for planning and research.

22. A **professional association** having all officers across the nation as members does not exist. Unlike many other countries, America has chosen not to regulate mandatory membership of a single, nationwide police association. Instead, a variety of specialized, voluntary associations promote their view of professionalism. Though generally consistent, they are limited by the specific scope and membership of their association.

WHAT PROFESSIONALISM WILL MEAN

It is ironic that the answers to law enforcement's future are found through an understanding of the past. History is a great teacher. The police and government as a whole, have been reluctant to learn from the past. We frequently refuse to acknowledge that other facets of society carry out similar tasks in a more efficient manner than ourselves.

Because the police don't look to the past for guidance doesn't diminish the potential for improvement. It indicates the tendency of human nature to resist change. Police leadership must rise above this tendency and seize the vision of tomorrow.

Tomorrow's quest for professionalism should begin today. It must be born from a dramatic change of management. Agencies struggling in an atmosphere of fear and intimidation have little chance of attaining professionalism. As strict bureaucratic management is replaced with a participatory, people-oriented style, the path to professionalism will be clear. The preceding list of accomplishments may act as a road map to professionalism. It will be clearly within reach once the change in management occurs.

Professionalism will mean officers possess a thorough knowledge of the behavioral sciences and have the wisdom necessary to cope with the problems of tomorrow's youth, technology, elderly and all of society's needs. Society will demand a more professional police officer. Likewise, they'll be willing to pay for improved performance and service.

Professionalism will generate a new sense of pride and dedication for police organizations. New found loyalty, teamwork and cooperation should raise levels of performance and productivity. The quality of service provided citizens will be substantially improved.

Improved personal satisfaction, gratification and financial reward will attract some of the brightest and most qualified applicants our nation has to offer. A four year college degree shall be the norm instead of the exception. Officers can feel a new sense of pride when asked, "What do you do for a living?"

Making law enforcement a true profession is well within our grasp. Yet, it can't come about merely through good intentions. Professionalism will only occur through managerial change. Such change can only take place when there is an "active" commitment — a commitment that goes beyond simply agreeing or acknowledging there's a better way of doing things. It's a commitment that demands police executives rise above good intentions and set an example for all to follow.

REFERENCES

1. John Dorschner, "The Dark Side of The Force," *Tropic, The Miami Herald Sunday Magazine,* The Miami Herald, March 8, 1987, pg. 1-22.
2. Dave Baca, "Drug Testing," *The Thin Blue Line,* June 1986, pg. 3.
3. Robert W. Wennerholm, "Drug Screening Test," *The Florida Police Chief,* July 1986, pg. 23.
4. Edward J. Tully, "The Near Future — Implications for Law Enforcement," *FBI Law Enforcement Bulletin,* Quantico, VA, July 1986, pg. 1-4.
5. John Naisbitt, *Megatrends,* Warner, New York, New York, 1982, pg. xxii-xxiii.
6. John Naisbitt, *Megatrends,* Warner, New York, New York, 1982, pg. 249.
7. Walter L. Ames, *Police and Community In Japan,* University of California, Berkeley, California, 1981, pg. 151-154.
8. David H. Bayley, *Forces of Order — Police Behavior In Japan and the United States,* University of California Press, Berkeley, California, 1976, pg. 53-57.
9. David H. Bayley, *Forces of Order — Police Behavior In Japan and the United States,* University of California Press, Berkeley, California, 1976, pg. 57.
10. David H. Bayley, *Forces of Order — Police Behavior In Japan and the United States,* University of California Press, Berkeley, California, 1976, pg. 58-59.
11. Walter L. Ames, *Police and Community In Japan,* University of California, Berkeley, California, 1981, pg. 199-201.
12. Edward Cornish, *Social and Technological Forecast for the Next 25 Years,* World Future Society, Bethesda, MD., 1986, pg. 1-8.
13. United Press International, "Crimes of the Future: White-Collar, Less Violent," *The Orlando Sentinel,* Orlando, Fla., March 15, 1987.
14. The Chicago Tribune, "Attitudes Toward Women In Workplace Have Softened," *The Orlando Sentinel,* Orlando, Fla., March 12, 1987.
15. Valerie Oberle and Rick Johnson, from a speech to the 1986 Region IX Conference, American Society for Training and Development, Lake Buena Vista, Florida, September 24, 1986.

16. Jerry W. Gilley and Michael W. Galbrath, "Examining Professional Certification," *Training and Development Journal,* June 1986, pg. 60.

17. John G. Kester, "Too Many Lawyers?" *The Washingtonian,* Wash., D.C., Feb. 1984.

18. Craig Crawford, "Lawyers Flip-Flop on Self-Regulation," *The Orlando Sentinel,* Orlando, Fla., Feb. 1987, pg. A-18.

19. John W. Zick, "Self-Regulation of the Accounting Profession," *Vital Speeches of the Day,* Delivered in Tulsa, Oklahoma, April 25, 1985.

20. Rosemary Goudreau, "Ama Moves to Target Bad Doctors, Break up 'Brotherhood of Silence', " *The Orlando Sentinel,* Orlando, Fla., June 20, 1987.

21. Nancy C. Jurik and Michael C. Musheno, "The Internal Crisis of Corrections: Professionalization and the Work Environment," *Justice Quarterly,* Academy of Criminal Justice Sciences, Dec. 1986, pg. 457-461.

22. Rosabeth Moss Kanter, *The Change Masters,* Simon & Schuster, Inc., New York, New York, 1983, pg. 361-362.

23. Nancy C. Jurik and Michael C. Musheno, "The Internal Crisis of Corrections: Professionalization and the Work Environment," *Justice Quarterly,* Academy of Criminal Justice Sciences, Dec. 1986, pg. 467-473.

24. The National Advisory Committee on Criminal Justice and Goals, "Agency and Jurisdictional Planning," *The National Advisory Committee on Criminal Justice and Goals Report,* Wash., D.C., 1973, Standard 5.4.

25. Webster's *Ninth New Collegiate Dictionary,* Merriam-Webster, Inc., Springfield, Mass., 1985, pg. 266.

26. Norman E. Pomrenke and B. Edward Campbell, "The Southern Police Institute," *FBI Law Enforcement Bulletin,* The Federal Bureau of Investigation, Wash., D.C., Feb. 1987, pg. 11-14.

27. James K. Stewart, "National Criminal Justice Reference Service," *FBI Law Enforcement Bulletin,* The Federal Bureau of Investigation, Wash., D.C., July 1985, pg. 10-15.

28. Thomas J. Deakin, "The Police Foundation," *FBI Law Enforcement Bulletin,* The Federal Bureau of Investigation, Wash., D.C., Nov. 1986, pg. 1-10.

29. John R. Bonee, "Excellence In Leadership," from a speech delivered at Itasca, Illinois, March 8, 1985.

30. Noel M. Tichy and Mary Anne Devanna, "The Transformational Leader," *Training and Development Journal,* July 1986, pg. 27-32.

31. Michael LeBoeuf, Ph.D., *The Greatest Management Principle in the World,* G.P. Putnam's Sons, New York, New York, 1985.

32. Robert H. Guest, from a speech delivered to The Industrial-Business Management Club of Greater Bridgeport, Bridgeport, Connecticut, Feb. 14, 1985.

33. James R. Metts, "The Police Force of Tomorrow," *The Futurist,* Bethesda, MD., October 1985, pg. 31-36.

34. Sharon S. Tafoya, "Innovations in Law Enforcement: Perceptions and Practices," as presented at the Annual Meeting, Academy of Criminal Justice Sciences, Orlando, Fla., March 1986.

INDEX